with kindest regards

+ Ted

HANDS ACROSS THE SEA

WITH BIBLIOGRAPHY AND NOTES

My 2006

Scotland and the Church of England in America
during the Colonial Period

EDWARD LUSCOMBE

CONTENTS

Preface

Today as battles are being waged in the American Episcopal Church for the very heart and soul of our church, Bishop Edward Luscombe has written an absolutely fascinating history on the impact of Scotland on the episcopate in the New World. For over a hundred years the "Episcopal Church" in the Colonies had no bishops. Consequently all of the aspirants to the diaconate and priesthood from the Colonies had to make the hazardous journey by sea to Britain to be ordained. At the same time British priests were being sent to the new world, primarily under the episcopal authority of the Bishop of London and under the auspices of the Society for the Propagation of the Gospel (SPG).

During the time when there were no bishops, a battle was being waged for the very heart and soul for the Church that was to become known as the Protestant Episcopal Church in the United States of America. What Luscombe shows in his significant work is how the Scottish Episcopal Church ultimately helped shape the ecclesiology and missiology of this new church some 3500 miles away from the British Isles.

Luscombe demonstrates at the outset of Hands Across the Sea the different roles that Scottish clergy played in the colonies, be it in the Southern colonies, which included Maryland, Virginia, North Carolina, South Carolina and Georgia, the Middle Colonies, which included New York, New Jersey, Pennsylvania and Delaware, and Colonial New England which included Massachusetts (along with Maine, Vermont and New Hampshire), and Connecticut. These three geographical regions were very different in churchmanship, as well as in their political leanings. The Southern Colonies tended to be "Latitudinarian and Whig"; the New England region were primarily "High Church and Tory", the Middle Colonies were "a mixture of them all". Some of the Scottish Clergy who came during the 17th and 18th Centuries left a permanent mark on what the Church in this new nation would become.

What Luscombe does in this book is that he looks at several clergy who went from the Scottish Episcopal Church to the New World to serve in different parishes. As a result of his study, a radical contrast between the bishops of Scotland and England is drawn and secondly, the desire of the Colonies not to adopt the English model of episcopacy.

In England there was opposition to the appointment of bishops for the New World. With the restoration of the Church of England as the established Church, the bishop was still an officer of state and a member of the House of Lords; he still had certain powers of coercive jurisdiction. He was not so much a Father in God as a judge, entrusted primarily with the task of maintaining discipline and repressing disorder.

"The Establishment connection, the political involvement and the trappings of palaces and wealth had obscured the true nature of episcopacy". That aspect of the episcopate was not very attractive in the colonies.

The Scottish Episcopal Church provided a sharp contrast to the bishops in the Church of England. The Scottish bishops had no political power, no palaces, and "pitifully low stipends." The contrasts could not have been more sharply defined. The "non-conformists" or "dissenters" remembered only too well how they had suffered under the Establishment of the Church of England and hence there was a strong movement in the Colonies, particularly amongst the non-conformists, not to have an episcopate at all, or if there were to be an episcopate, it should be an episcopacy radically different from what had been experienced (and remembered) in England.

That being said, the Anglican colonists wanted to have a bishop. Luscombe very helpfully points out that there were three different perspectives amongst Anglicans about the nature of the episcopal office. These three views were esse, bene esse, and plene esse. That is, whether the bishop was essential for the very being for the Church which was the Anglo-Catholic position; or whether the bishop was important for the good governance of the church which was the Low Church position; or the "middle of the road" view, that the bishop was the "ideal and fullest form of government for the perfection of the Church". These three different perspectives ultimately became the foundation stone of the Episcopal Church in the three geographical regions in the colonies. Despite these different understandings, the one thing the colonists did not want to have was a duplication of the English episcopate.

While it was ultimately the Scottish Episcopal Church who consecrated the first bishop for the New World, it must be said there were some Archbishops of Canterbury who were sympathetic to the plight of Anglicans in the Colonies. Those Archbishops devised different schemes, but ultimately each plan failed. The different plans failed for a multitude of reasons, but primarily because it was not the will of the Parliament or the Monarchy to enable the Colonies to have their own bishop. There was a sense that the Church of England was either powerless or did not have the will to act herself to allow the Anglicans in the Colonies to have an episcopacy.

In 1771 the then Bishop of Oxford, Robert Lowth, preached the Anniversary Sermon for SPG. In his sermon, Luscombe argues that Lowth preached a "post-mortem on the treatment of the American Church". Lowth said that day that the colonists were being "deprived of the common benefit, which all Christian Churches, in all ages, arid in every part of the world, have fully enjoyed. The proper and only remedy hath long since been pointed out: the appointment of one or more resident bishops, for the exercise of office purely Episcopal in the American Church of England". However good the intentions were of some in the Church of England, bishops and episcopal oversight in the Colonies was not going to be provided by England. That would not change until after the Revolution when the Scottish Episcopal Church would consecrate Samuel Seabury, something the Church of England would ultimately refuse to do.

Samuel Seabury was chosen by the clergy of Connecticut in 1783 to be their bishop. It was the desire of Seabury and Connecticut that their bishop should be consecrated by the Archbishop of Canterbury, but when Seabury arrived in London on 7 July 1783, he received a "cordial" welcome from Robert Lowth who was now the Bishop of London, but not such a warm welcome from either Canterbury or York. Lowth refused to take the lead and the then Archbishop of Canterbury, John Moore, was unwilling to support the appeal from Seabury and Connecticut. After an hour and a half meeting, all the hopes of an English consecration of Seabury ended in vain. I remember well Archbishop George Carey pointing to the portrait of Archbishop John Moore in the Guard Room at Lambeth Palace during his archiepiscopacy and lamenting, "this man refused to take a risk!" After being turned down by the Church of England, Seabury went to present his case in Scotland.

In Scotland, Seabury found a welcoming Primus in the person of Robert Kilgour, and although there was some hesitation on the part of some of the bishops in Scotland, the date of 14 November 1784 was set for Seabury's consecration with Bishop Arthur Petrie of Moray and Bishop John Skinner of Aberdeen being the co-consecrators with the Primus. The rest is history.

The Church of England would consecrate the next two bishops for Pennsylvania (William White) and New York (Samuel Provoost) in 1787, but even then the Church of England did not want White and Provoost to consecrate other bishops with Seabury because they "thought it more advisable that the Line of Bishops should be passed down from those who had received their commission from the same source."

It was not until 1792 when White said he would not take part in the consecration of the Revd Thomas John Claggett unless Seabury was episcopally included in the service that the episcopal line in America was established. "Of this sorry episode on the part of the English Establishment, Dr. William Jones Seabury [wrote] … "Through Bishop Claggett every Bishop since consecrated in the American Episcopate traces his line of Episcopal succession; and thus every one of those Bishops derives his Episcopate from the Scottish line as well as from the English Line."

It is frequently said that with the consecration in Aberdeen of Samuel Seabury, the Anglican Communion was born. Now some 221 years after that historic event, what was created that day is still taking form. Scotland still sees itself (as indeed it is) as an autonomous Province in the Anglican Communion, willing to act independently of the Church of England. Recently this has been true with the decisions made by the Bishops and Synod of the Scottish Episcopal Church with regard to the ordination of women to the priesthood and episcopacy and most recently the Statement issued by the Scottish College of Bishops in their response to the Windsor Report.

It is out of this lineage that the Protestant Episcopal Church in the United States of America was born. The Church in the United States is indebted to the Scottish Episcopal Church for its birth. It was from that birth that the Episcopal Church has the spirit of its mother as ECUSA participates in the Anglican Communion today.

The Revd Canon John L. Peterson
Canon for Global Justice and Reconciliation
The Washington National Cathedral

Secretary General of the Anglican Communion 1995-2004

Lent 2006

Chapter I
INTRODUCTION

On Sunday, the fourteenth of November 1784, three bishops of the impoverished Episcopal Church in Scotland consecrated an American priest as a bishop in the Church of God. The episcopal ordination of The Revd. Dr. Samuel Seabury of Connecticut took place in the upper room of Bishop John Skinner's house in Long Acre, Aberdeen. It was a notable waymark in the history of both the American Church and the Anglican Communion. The date is now commemorated in the calendars of the American, Canadian, South African and Scottish Prayer Books, although only recently in that of the Church of England.

The consecration, in fact, was the culmination of a very considerable contribution that the Scots had made to the developing Church in America during the preceding century. The most striking example of this was in Virginia. Of the one hundred and seventy-four priests who served in that colony, from 1723 until Independence in 1776, no less than forty-six were graduates of Scottish Universities. In addition to these there were some half-dozen others who were born in Scotland or came of Scottish descent.[1] Part of the reason for the disproportionately large part played by Scottish clergy had its origin in the political and ecclesiastical history of Scotland before and after the Revolution of 1668 which brought William and Mary to Britain. Part, too, lay in the political and ecclesiastical conditions in the American colonies.[2]

The century that followed the arrival of William and Mary marked the darkest period in the history of the Scottish Episcopal Church. It saw the disestablishment of episcopacy; the persecution of some of the priests – particularly in the south-west of Scotland; disabilities were later imposed upon men in Scottish orders, and penal laws passed which aimed at suppressing Episcopalian worship. Those factors all combined to drive many of the clergy from Scotland. Some of them crossed the Atlantic to a land where they could find freedom to continue the exercise of their ministry.

The following chapters tell something of their part in the developing Episcopal Church in America, and something, too, of the events surrounding the consecration of Samuel Seabury.

Chapter II
CHURCH AND STATE IN SCOTLAND
1560 TO 1788
REFORMATION TO REVOLUTION

The Reformation for Scotland began in 1560 with the severance of the official links between the Old Church and the Papacy, and with Roman Catholicism ceasing to be the established faith.

The Reformation Parliament of that year, whilst abolishing all authority derived from the Pope, did not abolish the office of a bishop. The First Book of Discipline (1560-1561) – a "Book of Reformation" commissioned by the Government – provided for superintendents rather than bishops, and for a time the two existed side by side. A Convention of the Estates held at Leith in 1572 restored episcopacy, but in name only, clergy bearing the title of bishops not having received episcopal ordination.[1]

Shortly after the Leith Convention, however, Andrew Melville, successively Principal of Glasgow University and of St. Mary's College, St Andrews, and often called the Father of Presbyterianism, led a movement opposed to both superintendents and bishops. In 1575 there began the long controversy between Episcopalianism and Presbyterianism in the Scottish Church which was to last until 1690. The Presbyterian system achieved statutory recognition from 1592 until 1610, when the Episcopal succession was recovered by the consecration of three Scottish clergy by bishops of the Church of England.

The Episcopalian regime was followed in 1638 by another Presbyterian interlude lasting until 1661, when the Episcopalian succession was once again received from bishops of the Church of England, and this was the regime until 1689.[2] It had fallen in 1638 because of its association with the administration of Charles 1, which was unpopular on constitutional as well as ecclesiastical grounds. It fell in 1689 because the Scottish bishops declined to renounce their allegiance to the Roman Catholic James VII, when he was dispossessed by William of Orange. The Convention of the Estates, under its newly assumed designation of the Parliament of Scotland, met in 1690 and passed an Act under which Presbyterian government finally became the government of the established Church of Scotland. Up until then there had, in effect, been two parties within one Church. Now there were two separate Churches, and the Episcopal Church had begun its own distinctive history.

But it was by no means a clear-cut or immediate affair. More than a hundred Episcopalian clergy in the west of Scotland had already been forcibly ejected from their churches during the winter of 1688-1689.

Even so, as late as 1707 there were a hundred and sixty-five Episcopal clergy in Scotland still in possession of their parishes and in receipt of stipends. In other places, Presbyterian ministers were being thrust into congregations which did not want them, sometimes having to break down barricaded doors in order to gain access to church buildings. This was particularly the case on the east coast north of the Tay, where Episcopacy continued strongly well into the eighteenth century. As an example, Gideon Guthrie, who became Episcopal minister of Brechin in 1711, noted in his Memorial (Brechin, 1712) that there were more than twelve hundred communicants at his first Easter service there. The Black Book of Kincardineshire (Stonehaven, 1841) recorded that when the Duke of Cumberland gutted the Episcopal Chapel in Stonehaven in 1746, there were "not above a dozen Presbyterians of the old Town".3

There have been various estimates of the relative strengths of Presbyterians and Episcopalians at the time of the 1690 Act. There is certainly ample evidence, even from Presbyterian sources, that the latter were the stronger. Alexander Carlyle, Parish Minister of Inveresk from 1748, wrote (in Autobiography, Chapter Vl): "When Presbytery was re-established in Scotland at the Revolution after the reign of Episcopacy for twenty-nine years, more than two-thirds of the people of the country, and most of the gentry were Episcopals."4

Whilst the numbers cannot be stated with any kind of mathematical accuracy, the broad facts appear to be that a/ the whole country north of the River Tay was predominantly Episcopalian; b/ between the Tay and the Forth the numbers were probably about equal; and c/ south of the Forth, Presbyterians were in the majority, particularly in the south-western counties where the Cameronians were congregated.

THE YEARS IN THE WILDERNESS

The next hundred years, until the Repeal of the Penal Laws in 1792, have often been described by Episcopal Church historians as "the wilderness years". Appealing to Scripture and to Christian antiquity, whilst retaining the historic creeds, sacraments and the threefold ministry of bishops, priests and deacons, the disestablished and disendowed Episcopal Church firmly claimed to be the Catholic and Reformed remnant of the Church of Scotland.

The 1690 Act had split the Church in Scotland in two, establishing Presbytery and leaving Episcopacy unestablished. But the Episcopalians were themselves split, not on theological but on political grounds. Whilst some of them were eventually willing to accept the rule of William and Mary, Anne and the Hanoverians, others, the non jurors, who were Jacobites continued to adhere to the exiled James Vll, seeing no future in anything but a restoration of that branch of the Stuarts. Under Queen Anne, there came an Act of Toleration in 1712, but that simply formalised the division and made it deeper. The Act gave protection to Episcopalians who were prepared to take an oath of allegiance to the reigning monarch and at the same time abjure the Stuart line and the Pretender. They were given freedom to worship according to "the Liturgy of the Church of England". From this sprang the "Qualified Congregations", qualified by having conformed to the requirements of the Act of Toleration. Because they used the English Prayer Book contained many English immigrants amongst their membership were not recognised by the Jacobite bishops and therefore of necessity recruited their clergy from England or Ireland, they were commonly referred to as the "English Church". These Qualified Congregations increased in number and in strength as the eighteenth century went on, particularly in the Lowland Towns. So much was this so, that by 1800, when Jacobitism was obviously a lost cause, they were roughly equal in numbers to the congregations of the Scottish Episcopal Church.[5]

If the story of the Qualified Congregations was of increase, that of the Jacobite non-jurors was one of decline The risings of 1715 and 1745 both ended in failure, the former after Sheriffmuir and the latter on the battlefield of Culloden. Both had been supported zealously by Episcopalians, non jurors, who were to pay a heavy price for their loyalty to the Stuart cause. After the 'Fifteen it was made illegal, on pain of imprisonment, for their clergy to hold a service for more than eight persons. Legislation after the 'Forty-five reduced that number to four, and imposed penalties on lay people who attended illegal services. Even more repressive measures in 1746 and 1748 made it impossible for any Presbyter ordained by a Scottish bishop to qualify for toleration, a blatantly obvious official attempt to extinguish native Scottish Episcopacy.[6] Whilst these severe statutes were not consistently enforced, they did result in a drastic decline in the numbers of non jurors throughout Scotland.

It has to be said that the bishops of the Church during the first half of the eighteenth century were not endowed with any great gifts of leadership, although they did have men of real learning amongst them, notably Thomas Rattray of Dunkeld (1684-1743) an outstanding liturgist and patristics scholar. They managed, however, to argue amongst themselves on a variety of matters. One of the principal of these was the election of bishops. Some held that the power to nominate to a vacant see was purely to preserve the episcopal succession. Agreement was finally reached that bishops should be elected by the clergy of the diocese, subject to confirmation by the existing bishops. The office of archbishop was allowed to lapse, to be replaced by the ancient office of Primus. In 1847, the fourteen pre–1690 dioceses were reduced to seven and allocated amongst the bishops.

There were disputes, too, over various liturgical practices, including the use of chrism in Confirmation and the practice of mixing a little water with the wine for Holy Communion – the so-called Usages.[7] The production of a Scottish Liturgy in 1764, and the eventual acceptance by the non-jurors of the Usages, added theological factors to the distinction between the non-juring and Qualified Congregations which had hitherto been almost entirely political.

The death in 1788 of Prince Charles Edward Stuart, for whom the non jurors had prayed as King Charles the Third, practically signalled the end of Jacobitism. His only heir was Prince Henry of York, who was a Cardinal of the Roman Catholic Church. It was now possible for non-jurors to pray with a clear conscience for King George the Third. But the Scottish Episcopal Church, apart from the Qualified Chapels, by this time had been reduced to what Sir Walter Scott in Guy Mannering called the "the shadow of a shade".[8]

Some, if not all of the blame must lie at the door of those bishops of the time who, in the words of Bishop Frederick Deane of Aberdeen (1868-1952), "linked the fortunes of the Church to a dying dynasty, and brought it down to ruin for the sake of a king who had fled his country and 'lost three kingdoms for a Mass!' On the other hand, they did hold firmly to the deposit of Evangelical Truth and Apostolic Order with an adamantine loyalty; their theology was the theology of the Caroline divines – and they did hand down to us that priceless heirloom, our Scottish Liturgy."[9] It was this Church, too, which consecrated Samuel Seabury in 1784 as the first bishop of the American Episcopal Church, thereby making one of the most significant of all contributions to the development of what was to become the world-wide Anglican Communion.

THE CONSEQUENCES

The years between 1688 and 1864 when the Episcopal Church had been subject firstly to repressive, then to penal and finally to restrictive legislation had a number of consequences, not only for the Church itself but indirectly for the development of the Anglican Communion.

NUMERICAL CONTRACTION

One inevitable result was the decline in numbers. From fourteen bishops, more than a thousand clergy and a majority of the population, (there were no statistical returns in 1688), the numbers had fallen to four bishops, forty clergy and less than ten thousand members a hundred years later.[10] Recovery began with the repeal of the Penal Laws in 1792, and by the time of the third Lambeth Conference in 1888, there were seven bishops. two hundred and fifty-one clergy and eighty-one thousand members.[11] The Scottish Episcopal Church had become a recognised and vigorous voice in the deliberations of the Anglican Communion, towards which Scots had made such a distinctive contribution.

The decline in numerical strength was matched by a similar drastic decrease in the material resources of the Church. To disendowment had been added the havoc wrought by the "rabblings" in the south west, and the kind of treatment meted out to the Kincardineshire church buildings by Cumberland's troops in 1745-46.

Against none of this was there any legal redress or compensation. The number of buildings began to increase in the 19th century. Charles Wordsworth, the Bishop of St. Andrews, could say to his Diocesan Synod in 1868, that "of the thirty-seven churches or chapels of all kinds now in the Diocese. all except two (Blair Atholl and Kirriemuir) had been built, or otherwise acquired, since the beginning of the present century".12

The poverty of the Church, the destruction of so many church buildings and the restrictions placed on Episcopalian worship all had their practical effects. Disendowment and the reduction in numbers meant that it was impossible to maintain the stipends of many of the clergy. Those who continued to be employed received only the smallest of stipends and lived in houses commensurate with their income. The bishops were compelled to combine their episcopal office with that of an incumbency in order to support themselves. This was a practice emulated by the bishops of the American Episcopal Church in its early years. In fact, on purely material grounds, there was little incentive for a young man to enter the ordained ministry of a Church whose future was hazardous and whose service was at best ill-paid. Nevertheless, it was precisely this apostolic poverty that evoked the admiration of the American Episcopalians.

ERASTIANISM

Perhaps the most important consequence of the years following 1688 was the total eradication of that ascendancy of State over Church known as Erastianism. At the time of disestablishment, the bishops virtually withdrew into private life, so much so that Viscount Dundee spoke of them as "the kirk invisible". They were waiting in the vain hope of the return of James VII with whom they kept in constant contact. After his death, they regarded themselves as continuing to hold office from his son, the Chevalier. By this time, most of them were old men, and in order to preserve the episcopal succession, they consecrated other bishops, without any specific jurisdiction over a diocese – the so-called "College Bishops".

When the last of the old line, Bishop Rose, died in 1720, the remaining bishops agreed that the whole Church should in future be governed by the College of Bishops acting together, without any single bishop having jurisdiction over his own diocese. One of their number would be Primus without any metropolitical jurisdiction, the theory being that the College of Bishops as a whole exercised that jurisdiction. The first part of this arrangement soon led to disagreement amongst the bishops, some of whom wished to return to the old diocesan pattern. The Chevalier's agents did their best to encourage continuance of the College Bishops, in the belief that the Episcopal Church would in this way remain more amenable to his party. However, the advocates of a return to the diocesan system won the day.

The issue was resolved by the bishops in 1727. They met in Edinburgh and drew up six Canons which provided the groundwork for the Code of Canons by which the Episcopal Church in Scotland is still governed. Most significantly, they spelled out the right of the clergy in a diocese to elect their own bishop, subject to the consent of the Primus and the remaining bishops.[13] The American Episcopal Church followed the pattern of a Primus – they resolved on having a presiding bishop without archiepiscopal authority, and this is still the practice. They followed the Scots, too, in having co-adjutor bishops with the right of succession when the diocesan bishop retired or died.

The 1727 meeting in Edinburgh was a turning point, not only for the Episcopal Church in Scotland, but for the future of Anglicanism. For the Scots, it was a recognition for the first time that the Church had a right to order its own affairs and appoint its own bishops, without waiting for a royal or governmental fiat. Having begun the progress, the Episcopal Church went on to develop from a body which had been crippled and almost destroyed by its loyalty to an exiled Prince, to become a church which had the vision to consecrate Samuel Seabury for the Americas in 1784 and Matthew Luscombe for Europe in 1825. It had discovered the meaning of "a free, valid and purely ecclesiastical episcopate".

Recognition of that situation was not so readily accorded by the Church of England. It was not until after the first meeting of the Lambeth Conference in 1867, that Robert Eden, the Scottish Primus, could say of that meeting "it for ever dissipated erroneous notions that the Church of England could not recognise any man for a true Bishop who was not made so by the authority of the Sovereign. In this assembly, one-third at least of the Bishops present were not so made, nor was any distinction recognised between the Bishops of an established or unestablished Church, all sat mingled together, all were alike equal as parts of the one Episcopate. Nor could the fact be passed over, which testifies to a principle of the first importance in considering the question of the renewal of intercommunion between different Churches, that the existence of different liturgies in Churches is no bar to their intercommunion".[14] Eden was premature in his report, for the Archbishop of York and the bishops of that Province had refused the invitation to attend the first Lambeth Conference. Even forty years later, Hensley Henson (then a Canon of Westminster, later Bishop of Durham) was to describe as "patently absurd" the notion that "Lebombo is the equal of London, Zululand pairs with Durham or Winchester" .

The 1727 meeting of the Scots bishops had a far-reaching effect upon the Anglican Communion outside England, however. It laid down a precedent for what has become widespread in virtually every other Province. This point is made by P H E Thomas in an essay in Authority in the Anglican Communion. After spelling out the way in which newly independent Anglican Provinces made provision in constitutional form for the proper management of their affairs, he goes on:– "Although aware that they were breaking new ground as far as the Church of England was concerned, the colonial Churchmen were not acting without precedent. The association of the

Scottish Episcopalians under canons after the year 1727 provided the first example of constitutional and synodical Anglicanism, and the North Americans used this example to develop their own ecclesiastical ideals in the atmosphere of newly-won independence. Victorian bishops of the overseas dioceses were well aware of these events, and Bishop Selwyn of New Zealand, a leading spokesman for the colonial Churches in the mid-nineteenth century, was in regular contact with leaders of the American Church at critical points of his career. The colonial Churches followed suit".[15]

THEOLOGICAL EDUCATION AND MINISTERIAL TRAINING

The Act of 1690 which required the principals and staffs of the Scottish Universities to subscribe the Westminster Confession and submit to Presbyterian government had resulted in the Episcopalian professors and lecturers being deprived of their posts. Any hopes of the Act being rescinded after the accession of Queen Anne were dashed when the Act for the Security of the Church of Scotland was passed in 1707. This provided that "in all time coming no Professors, Principalls, Regents, Masters or others bearing office in any University, College or School within this kingdom be capable or be admitted or allowed to continue in the Exercise of their said functions but such as shall own and acknowledge the Civill Government in the manner prescribed ... As also they do now and shall acknowledge and profess and shall subscribe the foresaid Confession of Faith as the Confession of their faith, and that they will practice and conform themselves to the worship presently in use in this Church and submit themselves to the Government and Discipline therefore ... "[16]

The practical effect of all this was that Episcopalian ordinands no longer read theology in the Scottish Universities. For the next two hundred years or so, the number of Episcopal clergy who had graduated in divinity could be counted in single figures. On the other hand, many of them continued to read for the degree of Master of Arts.

A sound knowledge of theology was still required, however, and made the subject of Canon law. The Canons of 1743 required ordinands to be "diligent students of the Scriptures, and of the fields of the apostolic and next two ages, that the people may be instructed in the truly Catholic principles of that pure and primitive Church." These requirements were elaborated and extended in subsequent revisions of the Canons.[17]

By contrast, the Church of England for many years had no specific theological requirements for ordination – as often as not Oxford Greats or its equivalent sufficed for a man to be made a deacon. Bishop John Hobart of New York, on a visit to Britain in 1824, remarked that "whilst the best educated amongst the English clergy were well versed in scholarship or in divers branches of science, they were commonly ignorant of the theology and history of the Church".[18]

In order to comply with the Scottish Canons, and to make up for the fact that ordinands no longer read divinity in the Scottish Universities, a different system of training was devised. A small theological school would be set up in the house of a scholarly priest. Most notable amongst these were John Skinner of Linshart (poet-priest and father and grandfather of Bishops of Aberdeen); Arthur Petrie, incumbent of St George's at Folla in Aberdeen and Bishop of Ross for a quarter of a century; and Alexander Jolly, who carried on the work after Petrie's death and who was Bishop of Moray from 1789 to 1838. In these small seminaries, a young man would receive his theological training, and – perhaps more importantly – be instructed in pastoralia whilst living a disciplined spiritual life.

One of Bishop Jolly's parishioners at Fraserburgh was Miss Kathrein Panton who in 1810 left a sum of money "to erect and endow a Seminary of Learning or Theological Institution for the education of young men desirous to serve in the Sacred Ministry of the Scottish Church." For some years, the College had a peripatetic existence in Edinburgh, followed by a spell of twenty-nine years at Glenalmond, eventually returning to Edinburgh and finally settling into Coates Hall in 1891.[19] Its foundation in 1810 made Edinburgh the oldest theological college in the Anglican Communion. It was followed by General Theological Seminary in New York City in 1817, and by Chichester Theological College in England in 1839. After that date, numerous other colleges opened in England and elsewhere. The method of instruction in Edinburgh followed on broadly the same lines, though more formally structured, as that conducted in the private homes of Skinner, Petrie and Jolly.

LITURGY

One important outcome of disestablishment was the opportunity that it gave the Scottish Episcopal Church to order its own worship and shape its own Prayer Book. The Church of England had no such freedom, since any alteration to its Book of Common Prayer of 1662 required the sanction of Parliament.[20] The Scottish Prayer Book, and particularly the form of eucharistic liturgy, indirectly through the American Episcopal Church, was to have a profound effect upon much of the Anglican Communion.

The first Scottish Prayer Book had been published in 1637, but had been used on only one Sunday before being withdrawn. The reason for the withdrawal was not so much its contents, as the manner in which it had been imposed. The virtual deprivation of the episcopate which the Episcopal Church suffered almost immediately thereafter and for nearly a quarter of a century, greatly impaired the unity of its liturgical tradition. It seems probable that every man did that which was right in his own eyes, so that not only was there for a considerable period no liturgical form that was considered as normative, but prayers and even the Holy

Communion service were commonly rendered in extemporary words. This is attested to by Thomas Rattray who wrote in 1740 "Let us now look back to the state of this Church with regard to public worship which indeed, at the Revolution and for a long time after, was very lamentable and hardly deserved the name; for we had no such thing as offices or liturgies among us".21 Rattray was largely responsible for the work which eventually led to the production of the Scottish Communion Office. Rattray's spiritual heir was Robert Forbes (Bishop of Ross and Argyll 1762-1777). Forbes was also a scholar and liturgist, and along with William Falconer (Bishop of Moray 1742-1777), he was responsible for the edition of the Scottish Prayer Book published in 1764. which was based on revisions of the earlier book. This was the edition that became the authorised Scottish Prayer Book and was to continue in use with minor alterations for the next century and a half.

The non-jurors in England had their own liturgy, finding that the English Prayer Book of 1662 was defective in its eucharistic expression. It was here that the Scottish Episcopalians were at one with their non-juring counterparts in England. There were primary distinctions between the Scottish and English orders for the Holy Communion. The first was the Epiclesis, that is "a prayer of Invocation for the descent of the Holy Spirit to bless and sanctify the Elements of bread and wine, to make them the sacramental body and blood of Christ". In this way, the prayer of consecration, it was claimed, was made thoroughly Trinitarian. The Epiclesis was absent from the English Communion Office. The other principal distinction was in the understanding that the consecration of the elements lay in the whole prayer, and not as in the English service, simply in the Words of Institution alone.

Despite these marked differences, however, both the English and Scottish offices bore clear marks of their common origin in that series of Prayer Books which had begun in 1549. It was in the language of the Scottish service that a high sacramental doctrine was made more explicit.

The importance of all this derives from the place of Books of Common Prayer within the life of Anglicanism. This is well expressed in an essay by Professor Louis Weil in The Study of Anglicanism:– "The Book of Common Prayer is for Anglicans far more than a collection of rites. Within Anglicanism the Prayer Book is a living expression of the profound union between what we believe and what we pray; a doctrinal document, not because it may contain such didactic materials as a catechism or historical documents of doctrinal significance, but because it is in corporate worship that Anglicans find the common ground for their profession of faith." The Book of Common Prayer played a part, not only in shaping Anglican piety but theology as well.22

The way in which the pattern of the Scottish Communion Office found its way into the American Episcopal Church through the Concordat between the Scottish bishops and Samuel Seabury is set out in a later chapter. For many American Episcopalians the contribution made by the Scots to Anglicanism in the form of that service ranks equally in importance with the consecration of Seabury as the first Anglican bishop outside the British Isles.

CLERGY LOSSES

The most serious consequence of disestablishment and the penal laws for the Episcopal Church was the loss of clergy and ordinands.

There were three particular pressures. The first was on those clergy who were forcibly and illegally ejected from their manses and churches in 1688-89 during the "rabblings" in the south-west of Scotland. Some crossed to Ireland, like the Inglis family, whose grandson became the first bishop in Canada after serving in the American colonies.

Then there were those who were deprived of their livings for refusing to take the oaths required by law, and who were legally, although sometimes forcibly, ejected. Many of those found their way to the American colonies, greatly helped by Henry Compton, the Bishop of London, and encouraged by James Blair, Compton's Commissary in Virginia, who had himself been deprived of an incumbency in the Diocese of Edinburgh.[23] George Keith, the first missionary of the Society for the Propagation of the Gospel had fallen into this category, although he was a Quaker at the time of his imprisonment.

The third pressure was on those who were discouraged from ordination in Scotland because of the restrictive legislation, even after the repeal of the Penal Laws. There was no great incentive to enter Scottish orders, since the restrictions ensured that a man's ministry would be confined to Scotland or to the Episcopal Church across the Atlantic. The act of 1840 "for granting relief to Pastors, Ministers and Lay persons of the Episcopal Communion in Scotland" afforded only marginal relief. The ninth section provided that "no person exercising the Function or assuming the Office and character of a Pastor or Minister of any Order in the Episcopal Communion in Scotland" was capable of holding a benefice, curacy or other spiritual promotion south of the border "unless he shall have been lawfully ordained by some Bishop of the Church of England and Ireland." The final disability was not removed until 1864.

The result was that many Scottish candidates for Anglican orders went to Oxford or Cambridge Universities, or else sought ordination from English bishops after graduating at a Scottish University. That was the only way in which they could exercise a ministry in England or in one of the colonies under the British crown. Some of them went to England on the advice of Scottish bishops. So, William Skinner, second son of Bishop John Skinner of Aberdeen, after graduating from Marischal College, Aberdeen, went to Wadham College, Oxford. He was then ordained by the Bishop of Rochester and served under Bishop Horsley of St. Asaph before returning to Aberdeen, eventually to succeed his father in the see.[24]

Dozens of Scots went to England to be ordained, and few ever returned to Scotland. Many went off to America, others to the four corners of the earth as pioneers in mission work. They were Scotland's loss, but their contribution to the developing Anglican Communion was immeasurable.

Chapter III
CHURCH AND STATE IN COLONIAL AMERICA
THE BACKGROUND

One of the principal areas to benefit from the exodus of clergy and potential clergy from Scotland was that of the colonies on the eastern seaboard of North America. In 1782, the British Government authorised their representative in Paris "to treat with the Commissioners appointed by the Colonys under the title of Thirteen United States." At the end of November of that year, a preliminary Treaty was signed, of which Article I read : "His Britannic Majesty acknowledges the said United States to be free, sovereign and independent States."[1] There had, in effect, been thirteen different countries, distinct in origin, in constitution and in religious practice.

From the 1570's onwards there were various English attempts to colonise the coasts of North America, but it was not until 1607 that the first group to survive permanently was settled in James Town (commemorating James I). This developed into the colony of Virginia, the name earlier given to the general area, and called after Elizabeth, the Virgin Queen. Thereafter other colonies developed, the last of the thirteen being Georgia in 1732.[2]

The northernmost colonies of New Hampshire, Massachusetts, Connecticut and Rhode Island became known collectively as New England. The so-called Middle Colonies consisted of New York, New Jersey, Pennsylvania and Delaware; whilst Virginia was included in the Southern Colonies with Maryland, North Carolina, South Carolina and Georgia. Broadly speaking, the Northern Colonies were Puritan, the Southern Colonies Anglican and the Middle Colonies predominantly neither the one nor the other. Their pattern of churchmanship reflected the differing origins of the colonists.

THE ECCLESIASTICAL PATTERNS
NEW ENGLAND

During the reign of Queen Elizabeth from 1588 to 1603, the Church of England became once and for all the official Church of the Land. Many radical Protestants in England were not satisfied that Church reform had gone far enough. In particular, they objected to the rites and ceremonies as remaining too similar to those of the Church of Rome, and they strongly insisted on the need for greater emphasis on the importance of the Bible and the exposition of the Scriptures. Because they wanted to "purify" the Church of England, they were given the name Puritans, a term at first used pejoratively, but later to become a matter of pride. Some of them – later called Congregationalists – wanted a totally de-centralised church polity – with members and their chosen minister being responsible only to one another. Others –

Presbyterians – wanted an organisation above the local congregation, with authority moving upwards from the local church and not downwards from above, as in the Church of England. Throughout the seventeenth century, increasingly repressive legislation made it difficult, if not impossible, for Puritans to worship in they way the believed to be right. Some went to the Continent of Europe, but they failed to find there the haven they expected. In 1619 some of these "Pilgrims" joined with others from England, sailing from Plymouth in Devon in the ship Mayflower. They intended to establish a Puritan settlement in Virginia, but the Atlantic storms drove the Mayflower further north than they had intended. The Pilgrims landed on the Massachusetts shore at Plymouth (named after their port of departure,) where they settled initially in conditions of great hardship. Their numbers were slow in growing, and even as late as 1650 there were still fewer than a thousand settlers there.

Then, in the summer of 1660, nearly a thousand more Puritans set out from England, to found Boston and other towns around. The Puritan Commonwealth had begun. Many other varieties of Puritanism followed, but only the admitted members of Congregational Churches were given the right to vote, despite the fact that the Massachusetts Charter required religious toleration. What had been denied to the early settlers when they lived in England they now denied to others in America. Quakers, for example, were banned from practising their faith.

As a result of this Puritan intolerance, allied with an increasing population, settlements radiated outwards. Rhode Island became a separate settlement where freedom of religion was allowed. So, too, did New Hampshire. But for Massachusetts and Connecticut the established religion was Congregationalism. By the end of the seventeenth century many of the excesses of intolerance were modified. Even so, forty years after the Pilgrim Fathers had landed at Plymouth, there was still no Anglican parish in New England. In fact, it was only the passage of the English Toleration Act of 1689 that brought religious toleration to Anglican residents of Massachusetts, and for another forty years after that, members of the Church of England in the Colony were still required to pay taxes to support the churches and ministers of the Congregationalist Standing Order.3

THE MIDDLE COLONIES

The situation in the Middle Colonies was very different from that in New England, once again reflecting the varied ethnic and religious backgrounds of the colonists. New York was first settled in 1610 by the Dutch. The original colony of "New Amsterdam", as it was called, included what was to become New Jersey. Because of the guarantee of religious toleration, it became a refuge for persecuted Protestants from France, Belgium, Germany and Bohemia. The war with Holland in 1664 changed it to a British possession, when it was granted to the Duke of York, from whom it derived its present name. At the beginning of the 18th century the population of the entire Province numbered only 25,000. A survey of the religious state of the colonists in 1701 reported that the Dutch, who were Calvinists, had some "Calvinistic congregations," the English, some of them Independents, had amongst them "many with no religions, like wild Indians". There appeared to be "no Church of England in Long Island, nor in all the great Continent of New York Province, except at New York Town".

New Jersey was first settled by Danes in 1624. They were soon followed by Swedes and Dutch – but like New York – the colony was acquired by the British in 1664 and granted to the Duke of York. In 1702 it became a Royal Colony under Queen Anne. The earliest English settlers were Quakers and Anabaptists. The population in 1701 numbered 11,000 and according to George Keith "except in two or three towns there was no place of worship of any sort," and people "lived very mean like Indians." Pennsylvania was originally settled by Swedes and Dutch. The area included what later became the State of Delaware. The Swedes surrendered to the Dutch in 1655, and the Dutch to the English in 1664. In that year, the colony was granted by Charter to William Penn, a Quaker missionary after whose family the territory was named. Penn considered the Colony to be "a Holy Experiment," giving freedom of worship to anyone who believed in "one Almighty and Eternal God". The first English settlers were 2,000 Quakers, who were followed from England by other denominations, including some members of the Church of England. By 1701 the population had risen to 20,000, most of whom were living "in the general neglect of the public worship of God", although the Swedes and the Danes were partly provided with ministers. The first Anglican congregation in Pennsylvania and Delaware was gathered in Philadelphia in 1694. Early in the 18th century, large numbers of Scots and Irish descended on Pennsylvania. They felt very little loyalty to the English government which had treated them badly back at home, and even less loyalty to the Anglican Church, since most of them were Presbyterians. Many of these later immigrants followed the valleys of the Appalachians into West Virginia and the Carolinas.[4]

THE SOUTHERN COLONIES

The settlers who landed at Chesapeake Bay in Virginia in 1607 saw the first celebration of the Holy Communion according to the use of the Church of England. It was in a makeshift church " a pen of poles with a sail for a roof, and for a pulpit a bar lashed between two convenient trees". The settlers suffered many vicissitudes – drought, hunger, malaria and, in 1662, the massacre of some of them at the hands of native Americans. Nevertheless, the Colony grew, fervently loyal to Crown and Church. Its Representative Assembly, (the first in America) enacted legislation to create an Established Church. Even when Cromwell's Commonwealth disestablished the Church in England, the Virginians remained steadfast. In 1641 the Governor of Virginia was instructed to be careful that Almighty God was served according to the form of religion established in the Church of England. By 1701 the Colony was far better provided for ecclesiastically than any other, the whole area being divided into some forty-four parishes, half of which had resident clergy to serve a population of 40.000. The parishes were run by groups known as vestries composed of twelve lay people – always white, and male, and usually wealthy. They had great power in appointing or dismissing clergy, as well as control of the fabric of the church buildings.

Maryland was first settled in 1634 under a Charter granted to Lord Baltimore, a Roman Catholic. Legally the Colony had to grant religious tolerance to members of the Church of England from the beginning, and from 1649, to all Trinitarian Churches as well. Like Virginia, the Anglican Church was comparatively well provided for. The Colony was divided into parishes, provision was made for stipends, and a regular supply of clergy provided. By 1700 there were fifteen priests holding parishes who attended a meeting in Annapolis with the Bishop of London's Commissary, Thomas Bray. The Church of England was made the Established Church of Maryland in 1702.[5]

South Carolina (originally united with North Carolina) was settled under a Charter granted to a Company in 1662. The objects of the Company were 1/ a desire to enlarge His Majesty's Dominions, and 2/ "zeal for the propagation of the Christian Faith in a country not yet cultivated or planted, and only inhabited by some barbarous people who had no knowledge of God". The first settlers arrived in 1670, most of these coming from the sugar plantations of Barbados, where slave labour was driving out small independent farmers. Charles Town (now Charleston) was founded in 1680. Another town sprang up in the Albemarle district, just south of Virginia, settled largely by people coming from that colony. Two quite distinct societies evolved – Charleston, prosperous with a thriving export trade, Albemarle poorer and more primitive. In 1712, the two were separated to form North and South Carolina. At the beginning of the 18th century, there was only one Anglican church (at Charleston), no schools and very few dissenting teachers of any kind.[6]

Georgia was established as an English Colony in 1732, with the object of creating a buffer between the southern Provinces of North America and the French and Spanish. It was also to afford an asylum to poor English families and to those Protestants in Germany who were being persecuted for their religion. The State was the scene of the labours of John and Charles Wesley.[7]

THE PROBLEMS

This was the vast area of mission with which Ecclesia Anglicana was confronted in the last quarter of the seventeenth century and for the succeeding hundred years.

It was a daunting task, not least because of the differing political and ecclesiastical conditions in the thirteen different States. A few Anglican clergy had crossed the Atlantic, some of them to accompany the settlers. Yet by 1669 there were still only four Church of England priests in the whole of North America outside Virginia and Maryland. In these two Colonies there were twenty and thirteen respectively – a total of thirty seven clergy altogether. Even as late as 1701, there were still only three Anglican churches in the whole of New England and the Middle Colonies – one at Boston, one at New York and one at Philadelphia.8

The fact that the appointment of clergy was in the hands of local vestries, that there was no bishop in America, no diocese and no central church authority, meant that all recruitment of clergy had to be done on an ad hoc basis. With no national newspapers, no Church Times and no Ecclesiastical Appointments Adviser in Britain, the difficulties were compounded.

The ecclesiastical jurisdiction of all clergy of the Church of England outside England was legally that of the Bishop of London. The natural corollary of this was that he was also ultimately responsible for the spiritual welfare of their people. Much would depend upon the attitude of the bishop and on his willingness to accept these new and increasing responsibilities.

The Anglican Communion owes much to the bishop who occupied the see of London in the crucial years from 1675 to 1713. His appointment of two outstanding priests as his Commissaries in the Colonies – James Blair of Scotland and Thomas Bray from England – was instrumental in ensuring that clergy were available to serve the American Church until Independence. Altogether, between some five and six hundred clergy served in what was then known as the Church of England in The Colonies. The bishop was Henry Compton.9

HENRY COMPTON
Bishop of London 1632-1713

In 1675, Henry Compton was translated from Oxford to become Bishop of London, where he remained until his death thirty-eight years later. It was a fortunate appointment for both the Scottish and the American churches. A son of the royalist Earl of Northampton, as a Tory, he was well aware of, and sympathetic to, the plight of the persecuted Scottish clergy. He was at one time accused by his critics of "taking much more care to prefer Scotchmen than the honest clergy of the Church of

England." And when a colonial governor complained in 1697 to Thomas Tenison, the Archbishop of Canterbury, that Virginia was being filled with Scottish clergy, Compton's reply was unequivocal: "Your Grace knows the circumstances of these poor men in their own country, but I must confess it both a charity to the men, and that it was a piece of good sense to the Plantations to send them further."[10]

He accepted his jurisdictional responsibilities outside England very seriously. He took for their basis, Richard Hooper's famous definition: "We hold that there is not a man of the Church of England but the same man is also a member of the commonwealth; nor any member of the commonwealth who is not also of the Church of England." It was natural extension that this should apply to subjects of the British crown who lived outside England.

This was supported by an Order in Council of 1633 which provided that:– "The Company of Merchant adventurers should not hereafter receive any minister into their Churches in foreign parts without His Majesty's approbation of the person, and that ye Liturgy and Discipline now in use in ye Church of England should be received and established there, and that in all things concerning their Church Government they should be under ye Jurisdiction of ye Ld Bpp of London as their Diocesan."[11]

It was this Order that was taken to be the authority for the jurisdiction of the Bishops of London over all overseas clergy of the Church of England. A later historian, however, has suggested that "the proper place to look for the origin of the precedent – for it had a basis no more definite or authoritative – on which the Bishop of London's jurisdiction rested, is in the Stuart policy instigated by Laud, of seeking to extend the Church of England Establishment to every part of the world where the English Government had a footing".

This was the slender legal foundation for the customary jurisdiction which Henry Compton inherited when he was translated from Oxford to London in 1675. Even so, Compton accepted responsibility for the spiritual care of the Plantations in North America with enthusiasm and disinterested zeal. A year after becoming Bishop of London, he was writing to a correspondent: "As to the care of your Churches with the rest of your Plantations which lies upon me as your diocesan, so to discharge that trust I shall omit no occasion of promoting their good and interest."

From the same year, 1676, there were clauses of identical effect to the 1633 Order written into the Instructions to Colonial Governors:¬ "60. You shall take especial care that God Almighty be decently and duly serv'd throughout your Government. The Book of Common Prayer as by Law estbish'd read each Sunday and Holy Day and the blessed Sacrament administer'd according to the rites of the Church of England ...

"61. You are not to prefer any Minister to any Ecclesiastical Benefice in that our province without a certificate from the Right Reverend Father in God the Bishop of London, of his being conformable to the doctrine and discipline of the Church of England ..."[64.]

And to the end the Ecclesiastical jurisdiction of the Bishop of London may take place in that Province so farr as conveniently may be, wee do think fit that you give all countenance and encouragement to the same, excepting only the collating to benefices, granting lycences for marriages and probate of Wills, which we have reserved to you, our Governor and to the Commander in Chief of our said Province for the time being."

Given the diversity of religious practices in the various colonies, the practical effects of these instructions were not great. An equal difficulty, of course, faced the Bishop of London. When, as he had discovered in 1675, there was a mere handful of Church of England clergy ministering in the "whole vast tract of America" it was not a matter of enormous concern. But the increase in the number of colonists, as in the number of clergy, made it imperative that some steps be taken. It was obviously impossible for a bishop who resided in England to be a true father in God to his American congregations or to exercise effective supervision over his clergy.

There was no bishop in any colonial church. It therefore became the responsibility of the Bishop of London to ordain men for work overseas as well as to issue licences for them to minister in some parish or chaplaincy. No one could officiate as an Anglican clergyman without his licence, and ordination candidates had to make the long, dangerous and expensive voyage to England to receive holy orders at his hands, or at the hands of some other English bishop acting under Letters Dimissory from him. Statistics show that about one in five of the American candidates died in the process of the journey to and from England.[12] The obvious solution, and one favoured by Compton, was the appointment of a resident bishop as a suffragan of London. However, as will be seen, this was not a solution that found ready acceptance in political circles at home, or with the Dissenters overseas.

Compton realised that if a suffragan bishop for America was impossible, some other local representation was essential. He therefore appointed a Commissary for the Crown Colony of Virginia where the Church of England was Established. A commissary has been defined as "an officer whom the bishops of the Church of England are accustomed to appoint to exercise ecclesiastical jurisdiction in particular parts of their diocese where, owing to distance or other causes, they cannot attend in person".

The nearest equivalent in England was probably an archdeacon, although there was some doubt as to the commissary's legal authority. In particular, he could not perform any so-called Episcopal act, that is, ordain, confirm or degrade ("unfrock") a clergyman. Compton's ideal was to have a commissary in every colony, but it was an ideal which he was never able to realise. In the meantime, Virginia was the ideal colony in which to start. The Bishop's choice was a vigorous, pious and able Scotsman, James Blair.

Chapter IV
THE SCOTTISH COMMISSARIES
EARLY YEARS

JAMES BLAIR
Commissary in Virginia 1689-1745

"The history of the Church in Virginia, over a period of fifty-three years during which he served as the commissary of the Bishop of London, is dominated by the life and influence of the one man" (Virginia's Mother Church – G. MacLaren Brydon, Richmond, 1945).[1]

James Blair was born, probably in Edinburgh, in the year 1656. He was the son of The Revd. Robert Blair, minister of Alvah in the Presbytery of Turrriff in Aberdeenshire. After two years as Crombie scholar in Greek, at Marischal College, Aberdeen, he went on to the University of Edinburgh, graduating M.A. in 1673 at the age of seventeen.

Six years later he was ordained by the Right Rev. John Wishart to the parish of Cranston in the diocese of Edinburgh, holding the charge for two years until he was deprived of the benefice for refusing to take the Test oaths.

Blair moved to England where he found employment as a clerk in the office of the Master of the Rolls, the head of the Civil Division of the High Court. He used his three years to good effect, making a number of contacts who were to stand him in good stead in later years. It was there that the Bishop of London first made his acquaintance. Impressed by Blair's ability and religious zeal, Compton offered him the opportunity to go to Virginia as a missionary. It was a challenge that the young Scots priest accepted, and with a licence from the Bishop of London, he went out in 1685 as Rector of the parish of Varina, later known as Henrico. It was frontier territory, to the west of the present city of Richmond, and still considered unsafe for settlement at that time because of its proximity to undisputed Indian hunting grounds. His first impression of this new country convinced him that there was much work to be done. He was horrified "not only at the disorderly and ineffectual condition of the Church, but the almost universal neglect of education".[2] When Compton appointed him as commissary in 1689, Blair had already had wide experience of Virginia. The office of commissary made him the highest ecclesiastical dignitary in the colony with authority to "supervise the clergy in a general way, to preside at the trials of the ministers charged with offences, and to pronounce sentence when they were convicted of crimes and misdemeanours". It gave him in 1694, a seat on the Council of the colonial government. Many years later, as the senior member of the Council, he was to act for several months as Governor of Virginia. In practice it was clear that Blair's effective authority would depend very largely on his powers of persuasion and his natural gifts of leadership. In his original instructions, Compton had warned him against "meddling with the laity" and advised him to "restrain the irregularities of the clergy". Twenty years later, in giving an account of his stewardship to Compton's successor, John Robinson, he wrote: "The chief of my business has been when I heard of any complaints of the clergy, first to try to reclaim them by monitory letters; and when that would not do, I have had a public visitation of the church, and upon an open trial of the facts have either acquitted or suspended the ministers, as the case required. I have made all my time but few examples of this kind; but I find it necessary not to be too slack, as on the other hand I am not suspected of too great severity".[3]

Immediately upon receipt of his Commission, Blair called together a convention of the clergy of the colony. This was held in Jamestown in 1690, and in its possibilities was the most important ecclesiastical meeting held in Virginia during the colonial period. It was to set a pattern for the regular conventions of clergy which were to become and remain a regular feature of the American Episcopal Church in the future.

The 1690 Convention in Jamestown had two principal items of business. One was a resolution to help in the establishment of a college in Virginia. The other was to begin the reform of abuses in the Church in the colony, and included the establishment of an ecclesiastical jurisdiction.

EDUCATION ADVANCE

The plans for a college were submitted to the Assembly, and Blair's petition was quickly and enthusiastically approved. Subscription lists were opened and substantial pledges obtained, with indications of widespread support for the project. Blair was sent to England in 1693 to obtain a charter and an assurance of continuing income for the college. His earlier contacts proved of great help in all this, and he secured an audience with the Queen and later with the King. The latter was impressed with the plan, telling Blair: "Sir, I am glad that the Colony is on so good a design, and I will promote it to the best of my power."[4]

The commissary returned to Jamestown, not only with the royal charter and provision for an assured income from the public funds, but also with a set of plans for the main building of the college as a gift from the architect, Sir Christopher Wren. Broadly speaking there were three aims in founding the College of William and Mary as it was now called. The first was the education of the children of the colonists, the second – the Christian education of Indian youth; and the third, provision for the training of young men for the ordained ministry of the Church in Virginia.[5]

The educational work began with a grammar school "for the immediate education of the youth of the said colony in the Latin and Greek languages". Blair had recruited in England a Scottish priest to be the first Master of the School. He was The Revd. Mungo Inglis, who began work immediately upon his arrival in Williamsburg, even before the buildings were completed. He served the College until his death in 1719, apart from an intermission when funds ran out. The school flourished under its Scottish master, and in due course became a degree granting body. By the end of the twentieth century, it had achieved a front-rank reputation in education.

The work with native American youth did not prosper as much as had been hoped. Blair had managed to gain the lion's share of the Boyle bequest – an annual grant to help in Christianising native Americans. This continued well, until the War of Independence severed the link with Britain; the Boyle money was then sent elsewhere and the Indian work finally ceased at the Revolution. Not a single native

American boy ever went through the college into the ministry of the Church. The majority of them returned to their tribes and to the ways of tribal life.

The third aim of providing locally-trained clergy was more successful, until the chair of theology was abolished and Thomas Jefferson directed that funds be expended on arts, rather than on theological subjects. Nevertheless, in the fifty years from 1723 until the Revolution, the College of William and Mary produced fifty five of the one hundred and seventy-four clergy who served in Virginia – more than the alumni of any other university of America, England or Scotland.[6]

M C Taylor in The Making of American Literature refers to Blair as "the creator of the healthiest and the most extensive intellectual influence that was felt in the Southern group of Colonies before the Revolution". Another historian echoes that assessment, "one must make profound and grateful recognition of the indomitable will and determination, and the great ability of the man who conceived the idea and carried it onwards through strain and stress to so great and abiding success. Virginia owes James Blair, President of the College of William and Mary, an undying debt of gratitude."

THE ECCLESIASTIC

After serving for nine years in Henrico, Blair moved to Jamestown, the better to supervise the College of which he became Life President. He combined the duties of an incumbent with those of a commissary. He was a man of restless energy and great ability. His initial intention of creating ecclesiastical courts did not materialise. Nevertheless, he saw the state of the Church in Virginia greatly improved.

He managed to fill vacant parishes with suitable clergy, many of them from Scotland. This did not gain him universal popularity. One of the colonists, Nicholas Moreau, a Hugenot clergyman, put the matter plainly in a letter to the Bishop of Lichfield ... "Though they have a great respect for my Lord Bishop of London, they do resent as a high affront to their Nation, because his Lordship has sent here Mr. Blaire, a Scotchman to be Commissary".[7] The objection of the then Governor, Sir Edmund Andros, to the Archbishop of Canterbury, 1697, that Blair was filling the country with Scottish clergy has already been referred to. It got short shrift from Compton and from the Archbishop. Andros was relieved of his governorship.[8] He was not the only one to cross swords with Blair, and on two further occasions the result was the replacement of the governor.

As well as filling many parishes with his fellow-Scots, Blair succeeded in raising and ensuring the stipends of the clergy. One other area where he managed to regularise matters was in the terms and conditions of appointment of clergy. The situation as regards vestries and clergy was described in his own words:

"In every Parish by the Law of that Country, there is a Vestry consisting of twelve men. The power of presenting Ministers is in them, but the Law in this point is little taken Notice of, by reason of the continuing Custom of making annual Agreements with the Ministers, which they call by a name coarse enough, viz: Hiring of the Ministers, so that they seldom present any ministers, that they may by that means keep them in more Subjection and Dependence. This Custom has had a great many bad consequences. No good Ministers that were informed of it would come into the country, and if they came, ignorant of such Custom they quickly felt the effects of it in the high hand wherewith most vestries manag'd their Power, and got out of the country again as soon as they could. The Mansion Houses, if there were any, went to Decay. The Minister holding the Living so precariously, that it could not be expected he would bestow much on Reparation, and very often the Glebe was not in his Hand. He stood likewise in so precarious terms that he must have special Care how he preached against the Vice that any great man of the Vestry was guilty of: for if he did, he might expect a faction would be made in the Vestry, to be against renewing the Agreement with him for another year. The Minister is dismissed at the Vestries' pleasure".[9]

It was the classic argument for security of tenure for a priest – the so-called "parsons freehold" of the Church of England. The commissary managed to enlist the help of the Assembly in going some way to rectifying the position, or at least, improving it. Nevertheless. vestries continued to be jealous of their rights vis-à-vis clerical appointments, and it is not surprising that the English bishops were later somewhat wary of the Constitution of the American Episcopal Church, in case it gave laymen and clergy too great a power in dealing with their diocesan bishop.

The administration of the Church of the Colony was greatly improved during Blair's time. He made systematic reports to the Bishop of London from which it is apparent that the pattern of Church life and clerical duty was not dissimilar from that existing in England at the time. There were quarterly communions, two services on a Sunday with sermons, care in visiting the sick and some instruction of the young, together with some pastoral care of the parishioners.

Blair died at the age of eighty-eight in 1743, having ministered in Virginia for no less than fifty-eight years, all but five of them as commissary for the Bishop of London.

"The story of James Blair is a story of pure and tireless labours. He was a man of great ability and force of character, very positive, very persistent, with an abundance of Scottish shrewdness, as well as Scottish enthusiasm, actuated by a lofty and apostolic determination to be useful to his fellow creatures, whether they liked it or not."[10]

ALEXANDER GARDEN
EARLY YEARS

One other Scot who held the office of Commissary for the Bishop of London was Alexander Garden. Born about the year 1685, he was a graduate of Marischal

College, Aberdeen, but unlike Blair he had received his ordination in the Church of England rather than in the Episcopal Church in Scotland. His first appointment was as a curate at All Hallows-by-the-Tower in the City of London.[11]

He was sent out to St. Philip's, Charleston in South Carolina in 1719. Almost co-incidental with his arrival, the people of that colony, dissatisfied with its proprietary government, placed themselves under the immediate protection of the king. Colonel Francis Nicholson was appointed as provincial governor.

He had earlier been governor of Virginia and was an ardent churchman and support of the Anglican cause. Garden had found St. Philip's uncompleted on his arrival in Charleston, but with the assistance of Nicholson an Act was passed for the finishing of the building. Under this, an additional duty was levied on rum, brandy, spirits and on slaves imported for sale – the proceeds to be used for building work.

Even so, it was not until 1733 that the church was finally completed.

An account of St. Philip's and its incumbent was sent to the Bishop of London in 1723 by the commissary, William Bull. It contained the following synopsis:–

"St Philip's, Charles Town. 300-400 Church families

A new church not entirely finished. A large regular

and beautiful building, exceeding any that are in his

Majesty's dominions in America. Mr Garden in charge

A learned and pious divine, but of a sickly and weak constitution"[12]

After seven years at St. Philip's, Garden received a commission from Edmund Gibson, who had become Bishop of London. Appointed commissary for North Carolina, South Carolina and the Bahamas "the learned and pious divine" entered upon this appointment with conscientious enthusiasm. And despite the "sickly and weak constitution" he combined the work of commissary with the rectorship of St. Philip's proving himself to be the most effective of Gibson's appointees, and to be far more assiduous in his duties than his predecessors had been.

ECCLESIASTICAL SUPERVISION

Garden examined the Letters of Orders and the Licences of all the clergy for whom he was responsible, and he listened to complaints by them and against them. The serious view that he took of his authority is revealed by the way in which he conducted ecclesiastical trials in strict canonical form. The Bishop had sent him instructions in Latin regarding the way in which this should he done in the case of irregular clergy within the American plantations, and Garden followed the directions conscientiously.[13]

He suspended four clergymen, of whom the most notable was George Whitefield, the evangelical preacher, and later Methodist colleague of the Wesleys. The charge against him was that he had failed to use the services of the Prayer Book when conducting public worship in the meeting-house in Charleston where he regularly preached. Whitefield declared his intention of appealing against the suspension. When the appeal failed to materialise, Garden suspended him in absentia, although the suspension did not appear to have had any practical effect.[14]

On the other hand, John Wesley on a visit to Charleston in 1736 recorded in his Journal his indebtedness to the commissary. The following year he was present at Garden's annual visitation and was deeply impressed by the quality of the South Carolina clergy. It was in Charleston in that year that Wesley published the first Anglican Hymnal in America – A Collection of' Psalms and Hymns. When Wesley was forced to leave Georgia after his trying experiences there, he was befriended by Garden and wrote of his deep gratitude for the kindness he had received.

On his appointment, the commissary discovered that the same practice of "hiring the ministers" on an annual basis was as prevalent in the Carolinas as Blair had found it to be in Virginia. He insisted that missionaries who had served one year in their post should either he given a permanent appointment or that the vestry should submit to the commissary in writing their objections to the priest. He managed, too, to regularise the stipends of the clergy and improve their rates and the conditions of their service. He was a good and forceful disciplinarian, but managed to retain both the affection and respect of the clergy. He had held the first of his eighteen annual visitations in 1730, establishing a pattern that was to continue until his resignation, when they were still carried on under the name of "annual meetings of clergy." At the first gathering, a programme was devised which was taken as a model for all subsequent visitations. They began with a public service at which one of the South Carolina clergy preached. This was followed by an address from the commissary – rather on the lines of a bishop's Charge. It invariably included an exhortation to pastoral care and fidelity in preaching the Gospel, then came a time for discussion with the clergy. These annual visits were greatly valued by the scattered missionaries.

Garden regularly submitted reports and accounts of his actings to both the Bishop of London and to the Society for the Propagation of the Gospel.

EDUCATION

Garden, like Blair, had a continuing interest in education, particularly in that of the children of slaves. He endeavoured to have a law enacted which would require the master of eighty or more slaves to have one of them trained as a schoolmaster to instruct the children on his plantation. This proposal did not meet with the planters' approval. In 1742, he proposed that the Society for the Propagation of the Gospel should appoint some of the clergy as its agents in purchasing slaves between the ages of twelve and sixteen who would be trained as catechists. The Society approved of the plan and asked Garden and two other clergymen to begin the experiment. In fact, Garden had already done this some time earlier. He had arranged for two boys aged fourteen and fifteen to be sent to school and they would in due course be used to instruct their fellows. Garden asked the SPG to reimburse him for the cost of what he had already undertaken – £59.9.½. The future would be his responsibility. Later, he reported on their progress. Both had learned to read the New Testament exceedingly well in the space of eight months. The school was duly opened with the boys as instructors. A year later it had doubled in numbers. The SPG sent out Bibles, Prayer Books and spelling books. The school in Garden's words "continued to send out young Negroes capable of reading the Scriptures and instructed in the chief principles of Christianity, who it is hoped. will diffuse their light and knowledge to their Parents, Relations, Country men and Fellow Servants". In 1747, the commissary wrote, "the school exceeds even beyond my first Hopes and Expectations". It continued to flourish for another twenty years, and that at a time when the Government of South Carolina did not have a single Institution for the education of the fifty thousand slaves in the colony.[15]

In 1748, feeling the advance of age, Garden resigned as commissary and five years later retired from the rectorship of St Philip's. He returned to Britain, but found the climate too severe and went back to Charleston, where he died at the age of seventy-one. He had spent thirty-seven years in South Carolina.

No one was appointed to succeed him as commissary. By that time Thomas Sherlock had become Bishop of London. It was Sherlock's deliberate policy not to appoint any new commissaries in the hope that it would force the British Government to consider more favourably the appointment of a bishop for the colonies. Of Garden, it was said that "none exceeded him in the hold and hearts of people, and none left a more lasting place upon the Church and community at large". His twenty years in office marked the consolidation of South Carolina's Anglican establishment. A twentieth century historian has written that Alexander Garden "shaped the Anglicanism of the colony more than any other figure."[16]

Chapter V
ARCHITECTS AND PLANNERS
THOMAS BRAY

The first commissary in the American colonies, James Blair. began his duties in Virginia in 1689. A second appointment was made by Bishop Compton six years later, this time of a commissary for Maryland. He was Dr. Thomas Bray, an English incumbent working in Warwickshire. However, it was not until 1699 that Bray was able to afford the passage, and only in December of that year that he sailed for America.

In the meantime, he had been busily engaged in recruiting clergy for the colony, and in making plans for Garden equipping them with adequate supplies of books. Like Blair and Garden he had a particular concern for education. Soon after his appointment in 1695, he had published a paper entitled Proposal for Encouraging Learning and Religion in the Foreign Plantations. He began a public appeal to further those ends, which eventually developed into the Society for the Promotion of Christian Knowledge (SPCK), the first meeting of which was held in 1689.

Bray arrived in Maryland early in 1690, and was, in fact only resident in the colony for three months. It was a period packed with an extraordinary amount of activity. and a time for gathering a great deal of information about the needs of the Church in Maryland and beyond. He tried to secure the stipends of the clergy; he made contact with people of real influence in Church and State; he tried to establish libraries; and he stamped his own authority upon the work generally.

In the midst of all this, he held a thirteen-day Visitation in May 1690 with the intention of

        a/ preventing scandals amongst the clergy
        b/ exhorting them to be faithful in catechising; preaching and teaching
        c/ propagating true religion in the provinces adjoining Maryland

Bray became convinced that he would better serve the Church in the colonies by returning to England and working from there. Events were soon to prove that his conviction had been right. He managed to persuade parliament and the king to pass an Act restoring a poll tax for the support of the colonial clergy . But, more importantly, he was instrumental in broadening the scope of the Society for the Promotion of Christian Knowledge. By 1701, a Royal Charter had been obtained for a new daughter Society – for the Propagation of the Gospel in Foreign Parts (SPG). It was a move of enormous importance for the future of the Anglican Communion. From that time onwards the Bishop of London was no longer solely responsible for the provision of clergy for the colonies, although he did, of course, retain his customary jurisdiction.

It was natural, particularly with Thomas Bray's connection with Maryland, that the newly formed Society should first turn its attention to the North American colonies. It was there that most of the overseas "loveing subjects of the king" were to be found. For the first eighty years of its existence, the Society's attention was given almost entirely to the colonies. although not exclusively to the colonists. SPG laid upon its missionaries the duty of caring for all whom they could reach, and many of them (including many Scots clergy) faithfully fulfilled that duty. The baptism of slaves and (although less often) of native Americans was frequently recorded in the Notitia Parochialis, a kind of summary statistical return.

From the time of its foundation until the independence of the thirteen colonies, no fewer than three hundred and seven missionaries had been supported there by the SPG. It was only because the Royal Charter restricted the Society's mission to work amongst "the king's loveing subjects" that support was withdrawn – Independence, of course having severed the links between monarch and subjects.1

GEORGE KEITH
First Missionary of the Society for Propagation of the Gospel 1702-1704

The SPG began its work in a most thorough way by making a survey of the needs that it had been created to meet. Letters of enquiry were sent out to the Colonies, to officials and to leading clergy. In addition, there were people at home who were able to give valuable evidence and advice. There was, of course, Dr. Bray himself. Bishop Compton of London handed in a comprehensive dossier on the particulars that he had of the clergy and of their work in the colonies. Particularly useful was the help of two colonial governors, Colonel Lewis Morris of New Jersey, and Colonel Joseph Dudley of New England, who happened to be on leave in England at the time of the survey.

Both Morris and Dudley were committed Christians and keen–eyed observers. Dudley submitted to the Society a wide-ranging survey of all the "English Plantations" from South Carolina to Maine. In the whole the New England provinces there was only one Church of England – that at Boston with two ministers. Virginia was divided into forty parishes, but lack of clergy had hindered progress. Maryland, he hoped, had been well supplied by Dr. Bray. Elsewhere – New York, New Jersey, Pensylvania. the Carolinas – with sixty thousand colonists, had no minister and almost no schools. Morris presented a similar picture and added a suggestion for providing suitable clergy – "Let the king, the Archbishop, the Bishops and the great men admit no man for many years to any great Benefice, but such as shall oblige themselves to preach three years gratis in America … By this means we shall have the greatest and best men".[2] It will be no surprise that this form of clerical conscription found little favour.

Perhaps the most useful advice of all for the Society's preliminary survey of needs came from a Scotsman, The Revd. George Keith. Taken with the evidence of Compton, Bray, Dudley, Morris and that from the colonies themselves, it all confirmed the need for vigorous and widespread help. Keith had far more knowledge and experience of the religious situation in the colonies than most other men, and he was eager to help. There could have been no better pioneer for the Society, and he was adopted as its first missionary on the 27 February 1702. Less than a month later, the second missionary was appointed in the person of another Scotsman, The Revd. Patrick Gordon.

George Keith was born in Peterhead, Aberdeenshire in 1638. He was educated at Marischal College, (where he was a contemporary of Gilbert Burnet, subsequently Bishop of Salisbury and notable church historian) graduating Master of Arts in 1658. He was a scholar of marked ability, particularly in mathematics and oriental studies and became a convinced Quaker under the influence of the Quaker apostle, William Dewsbury. Keith quickly became one of the foremost apologists of the central principles of the Quaker faith for which he suffered persecution, including a long period of imprisonment in the Tolbooth in Old Aberdeen. In 1671 he accompanied William Penn, Robert Barclay and George Fox on an extensive missionary expedition through Holland and Germany. On his return from the

Continent, Keith established a boarding school in Middlesex where he remained until 1685, when he was appointed as surveyor-general of New Jersey. Four years later he became headmaster of the famous school founded by William Penn in Philadelphia.₃ Keith became increasingly convinced of the place of sacraments in religious life, and eventually parted company with the Society of Friends setting up a separatist party of Christian Quakers, popularly known as "Keithians" or "Keithites". It was a serious defection from the point of view of the main body of Quakers, and efforts were made to effect a reconciliation. Keith returned to London in the mid sixteen-nineties and in 1700 was ordained in the Church of England by Bishop Compton. Two years later he had become the first missionary of the SPG, charged with making an on-the-spot survey of the state of the Anglican Church in the Colonies, and with making recommendations as to the needs to be met. By this time, he was sixty-four years old.

When Keith reported that he had hopes of a passage in one of Her Majesty's ships, the Society made active provision for his journey. They voted a sum of £200 for his actual travelling expenses, and another £200 for his wife and children as a kind of life assurance "if he dye". Another £50 was voted for literature to accompany him. He had to wait two months before embarking on a ship, and in the meantime the second missionary had been adopted.

The Revd. Patrick Gordon had been appointed by the Bishop of London to serve in New York. Like his fellow-Scot, he was an able scholar. He was the compiler of a Church Catechism which was adopted as the standard work for the Society. He was, too, the author of a Geographical Grammar, at the end of which he had made a strong plea for the conversion of the heathen. He had also prepared a scheme for the conversion of the native Americans, which he submitted to the Society, where it was received but not commented upon. Gordon's idea was to set up schools of charity boys on the edge of the Indian territories in the hope that the boys would make friends with Indians of the same age who would be then encouraged to join the schools. There they would be able to assimilate the language and ways of their civilised companions, who would in turn be "matched" with Indian girls. So, by a process of absorption and cross-fertilisation they would bring about the conversion and civilisation of the tribes. Once this was done, the schools would then be moved to other frontier areas and so the good work would proceed. It was a novel theory, but was to remain only a theory. The SPG let the proposals "lie on the table".4 But Gordon was not only a theorist, he was a practical man as well. After he had offered himself to, and had been accepted by, Compton. the bishop commended him to the SPG. The diocese of York had promised £50 towards Gordon's support, but the imminence of the passage with Keith prompted the Society to pay for the travels in anticipation of receiving the promised money from York. In addition, they voted Gordon the sum of £10 to pay for books and they sent him on his way with their blessing.

Keith and Gordon sailed from Cowes in HMS Centurion in April 1702. There was a third Anglican clergyman on board, The Revd. John Talbot, who was destined to play a significant part in the life of the American Church in the colonies. Talbot was the ship's chaplain and he listened avidly to Keith's plans about his mission, becoming so interested that he asked to join in the project. Keith agreed, sent home the proposal to the SPG who consented. and for two years the pair of them travelled through the colonies. proving ideal companions in the arduous journeying and preaching that lay ahead. Also on board, to the great benefit of the missionaries, were the two colonial governors who had earlier that year given evidence to the SPG – Colonel Dudley and Colonel Morris. Keith reported "that it was a very pleasant voyage. Relations were consistently very good with the governors, the captain. inferior officers and all the marriners generally. The great cabin of the ship was like a colledge for good discourse, both on matters theological and philosophical … severall of the seamen as well as the officers, joined devoutly with us in our daily prayers according to the Church of England, and so did other gentlemen that were passengers with us."5 Patrick Gordon went off to New York, where the Commissary had appointed him to the care of Jamaica in Long Island. Unhappily he contracted a fever "the day before he designed to preach, and so continued until his death – about eight days after." The Society's first missionary had given his life. He was the precursor of many more. Gordon's place was taken for a year by another Scot, The Revd. James Honyman. On Honyman's transfer to Rhode Island in New England, yet another Scot was appointed to Jamaica. He was The Revd. William Urquhart who spent five years in the charge until his death in 1709.

Meanwhile, Keith and Talbot set off on their journey around the colonies. Five months later, Talbot reported on their travels:

"Friend Keith and I have been above five hundred miles together, visiting the churches in these parts of America, namely New England. New Hampshire, New Bristol, New London, New York with New Jerseys, as far as Philadelphia. We preached in all the churches where we came, and in several dissenters' meetings. such as owned the Church of England to be their mother church, and were willing to communicate with her, and to submit to her bishops, if they had opportunity. I have baptised several persons whom Mr Keith has brought over from Quakerism; and indeed, in all places where we came. we found a great response and inclination amongst all sorts of people to embrace the Gospel. Even the Indians themselves have promised obedience to "that faith", as appears by a conference that my Lord Cornbury, the Governor here, has had with them at Albany. Five of their Sachems. or kings. told him they were glad to hear that the sun shined in England again since King William's death. They did admire at first what was come to us that we should have a squaw Sachem, namely a woman king; but, they hoped, she would be a great mother and send them someone to teach them religion … ."6

More than a year later, Talbot wrote to the SPG from Philadelphia:¬

"We have gathered together several hundreds for the Church of England. and what is more, to build houses for her service. That at Burlington is almost finished. Mr Keith preached the first sermon in it before my Lord Cornbury. Churches are going up amain where there were never any before. They are going to build three at North Carolina, to keep the people together, lest they should fall into heathenism, quakerism, etc. and three more in those lower countries about Newcastle, besides those I hope at Chester, Burlington and Amboy ..."

"Mr Keith has done great service to the Church, wherever he has been, by preaching and disputing publicly, and from house to house: he has confuted many, (especially Anabaptists) by labour and travel night and day; by writing and printing in books. mostly at his own charge and cost, and giving them out freely, which has been very expensive to him. By these means people are much awakened and their eyes opened to see the good old way and they are very well pleased to find the Church at last take such care of her children."[7]

At the end of his two year sojourn, Keith had covered all the colonies from Maine to North Carolina, a distance of eight hundred miles. He had visited many places twice and preached everywhere he went. Many of his old friends amongst the Quakers followed him into the church, as did numerous other Dissenters, including some ministers. With prodigious energy he and Talbot found out where there were enough church people to welcome and support a minister and build a church.

On his return to London, Keith prepared his Report to the Society. Talbot remained behind in America, and in response to the following request from two hundred families in Burlington, New Jersey, settled there in 1704; supported by SPG:¬–

"We desire to adore the goodness of God for making the hearts of the Lords Spirituall, Nobles and Gentry, to enter into a Society for Propagating the Gospell in Foreign Parts, the Benefit of which we have already experienced and hope further to enjoy. These encouragements caused us some time since to joyn in a subscription to build a church here, which tho not as yett near finish'd have heard many good sermons in it from The Revd. Mr Keith and The Revd. Mr Jno Talbot, whom next to Mr Keith wee have a very good esteem for and do in all humility beseech your Lordships that he may receive orders from you to settle with us. Our circumstances at present are such that wee cannot without the assistance of your Lordships, maintain a Minr."[8]

The SPG published Keith's journal after his return to England. The following is a summary of his travels:

"I have given an entire Journal of my two years Missionary Travel and Service, on the Continent of North America, betwixt Piscataway River in New England. and Coretuck in North Carolina, of extent in Length about eight hundred miles, within which bounds are Ten distinct Colonies and Governments, all under the Crown of England, viz, Piscataway, Boston (Colony called Massachusett's Bay), Rhod. Island (Colony included also Naraganset, and other adjacent parts on the Continent), Connecticut. New York, East and West Jersey, Pensilvania, Maryland,

Virginia and North Carolina. I travelled twice over most of those Governments and Colonies, and I preached oft in many of them. particularly in Pensilvania, West and East Jersey, and New York Provinces where we continued longest. and found the greatest occasion for our service."9

His report formed the basis of a strategy for mission by the Society. "The first phase was over; the field had been surveyed, the organisation erected and set going. The Society pressed forward with hope and determination." As for Keith himself he spent the last years of his life as Rector of the country charge of Edburton in Sussex frequently advising the SPG on North American affairs. An American historian has described him as "one of the great men of his age".10

Perhaps the final assessment of George Keith and of his contribution to the early colonial Church can be left to his fellow labourer, The Revd. John Talbot:–

"I look upon it that the sending of Mr Keith in quality of a missionary, to travel for the good of the churches, has been the best service that has been done yet for the Church of England in these parts of the world; for he is a general scholar, an able disputant, and a perfectly honest man ... He is the fittest man that every came over for this province: he is a well study'd divine, a good philosopher and preacher, but above all an excellent disputant. especially against the Quakers, who used to challenge all mankind formerly. Now all the "Friends" (or Enemies rather) are not able to answer one George Keith; he knows the depth of Satan within them and all the doublings and windings of the Snake in the Grass. In short he has become the best champion against all dissenters that the Church ever had, and he's set up such a light in these dark places that by God's blessing will not be put out ... "He has done more for the Church than any. yea than all that have been before him."11

Chapter VI
SPREADING THE WORD

The Society for Propagating the Gospel in Foreign Parts, following its consultations and study of the Report by George Keith, made it a matter of deliberate policy to send clergy only to those areas where there was perceived to be the greatest need. The view was taken that, for example, Virginia had been well served in the appointments made by James Blair, and that Maryland had been similarly well served by Thomas Bray's efforts. As a result, those two colonies between them received only seven men out of a total of three hundred and seven sent out by the SPG between 1702 and 1783.[1]

This policy was later changed to one of sending missionaries only to places where there had been an application from an organised congregation, or where an assurance was given that a church would be built and at least some contribution made towards the support of a minister. There were still seventy-seven SPG missionaries serving in the Colonies at the time of Independence, when the restrictive terms of its Charter compelled the Society to withdraw its support.[2]

The Society was not, of course, the only source for clergy. Some were recruited locally and as the eighteenth century wore on, an increasing number of these came from the College of William and Mary. Others, also locally recruited, came from amongst the tutors and schoolmasters who had earlier emigrated to the Colonies. Some of these continued to teach after ordination, combining it with their pastoral ministry. The Revd. Archibald Campbell (rector of Washington Parish in Westmoreland County, Virginia) for instance, was reputed to have had amongst the pupils in his school – Chief Justice John Marshall, Presidents James Madison and James Monroe, and probably George Washington, too.

The one common factor for all the colonial clergy was that they had invariably received their ordination at the hands of a bishop in the British Isles – a necessity because of the absence of any bishop in America. In every one of the thirteen colonies, clergy from Scotland or of Scottish descent were to be found serving as parish priests.

Most of these clergy worked initially under great difficulties, varying from the Puritan hostility in New England, to service in areas where the colonists had never heard the name of God or of Jesus Christ. There was also sometimes a particular prejudice against the appointment of an incumbent who was a Scot. Governor Andros of Virginia and Nicholas Moreau were not the only complainants. In 1706, the Governor of New York, William Burnet. reported that Thomas Barclay, the Chaplain at Albany, spoke with such a pronounced Scottish accent "as to be difficult to understand." When the congregation at Elizabeth Town, New Jersey wrote to the SPG in 1706, they asked that "the Society would be pleased to send one of the Church of England who is not a Scotchman".[3] Even as late as 1764, Governor

Horatio Sharpe of Maryland was writing: "I shall, according to your Desire, provide for The Revd. Mr Lowe who seems I think to be a decent and well-behaved Man. I wish he may preach as well as he looks and pronounce English a little better than the Generality of our Scotch clergymen who hold at present so many of the Benefices in the Province that near half the inhabitants have some Room for Complaint that they are obliged to pay their Minister for preaching to them in an unknown tongue". (David Lowe was the rector of All Hallows in Arundel County from 1764 until 1780 when he was forced out by the Revolutionary War).[4]

On the other hand, there was occasional praise. Shortly after George Keith had returned to England in 1704, John Talbot wrote to him about The Revd. William Urquhart, "Mr Urquhart is well chosen for the people of Jamaica (Long Island) and indeed I think none fitter than the Scottish Episcopal to deal with Whigs and Fanatics of all sorts".[5]

An outstanding feature of the colonial clergy was the length of time that many of them served in one particular parish. A rectorship of thirty years and more was a common occurrence. This is all the more remarkable in the light of the earlier practice of vestries "hiring the ministers" on an annual basis.

These chapters contain some examples of Scottish clergy who left their mark on each of the three geographical groupings of colonies. There were numerous other "which have no memorial" whose faithful ministry nonetheless did much to establish and develop the Anglican tradition in America.

There were two areas of mission, however, which did not fit neatly into the three geographical groupings. The first was Florida, and the other was the work done amongst the native Americans.

FLORIDA

Florida had only a short period of existence as a British possession prior to Independence, and was not one of the thirteen colonies that became the United States at the Treaty of Paris in 1783. It had had been ceded to the British Crown by Spain in 1763, at a time when the entire population of East and West Florida together numbered a mere seven thousand. Each of the two areas was placed under the jurisdiction of a governor. During the twenty years under British rule, a total of nine Anglican clergy were sent out. The SPG assisted in the recruitment and selection of these clergy, but undertook no financial responsibility either for their passages from Britain or for their stipends in America. Each of them received a bounty to defray the cost of travel, and each was paid a stipend of £100 a year by the Government of Florida. It was not at that time a particularly desirable place in which to work, and a handful of clergy became discouraged on arrival and sought pastures new. A clergyman of South Carolina told the Bishop of London: "The vacant parishes in this Colony are filled up by such Ministers as were sent out to

East and West Florida, and who disliking their Mission in those parts have removed and settled here. I believe it will be very difficult for some time to induce any of the clergy to reside in those infant Countries; where the Necessaries of Life are procured with great Difficulty, as well as purchased at the most exorbitant rate."[6]

Of the nine clergy who served in Florida, four were Scots – Forbes, Fraser, Gordon and Seymour. Fraser had a short ministry of three years from 1769 until his death in East Florida in 1772. Seymour (like Forbes, an Aberdonian) had a ministry of less than a year. Nevertheless, during that time he baptised ninety-four children, married thirty-three couples, and conducted forty-seven funerals. Gordon served in Mobile from 1767 until 1781, proving to be a faithful and effective minister. The most notable of all the clergy was John Forbes.[7]

Forbes was licensed "to the Plantations of East Florida" in May 1764 – specifically to St. Augustine. He was destined to play a prominent part – not only in the life of the Church, but equally in the administrative and judicial life of the province. Born in Strathdon, Scotland, he was educated at Marischal College, Aberdeen, graduating Master of Arts in 1755 and afterwards attended classes in Divinity.

He arrived in East Florida in priest's orders at much the same time as the first Governor, James Grant. Grant was a staunch friend of the Church. Almost immediately he appointed Forbes to a seat on the Council Board, an office he held for the whole of his time in the province. When the Spaniards had evacuated East Florida the previous year, they left unfinished their new parish church in St. Augustine. The governor, who had been empowered in his commission to "collate any Person or Persons to any Churches, Chapels and other Ecclesiastical Benefices", appointed Forbes to the incumbency of St. Augustine. The young Scottish priest began the exercise of an energetic and fruitful ministry which was to last nineteen years. In due course, the Church building was completed at St. Peter's, and a tower and steeple were added.

As well as his incumbency and his seat on the Council, Forbes became sole judge surrogate of His Majesty's Court of Vice-Admiralty, assistant judge of the Court of Common Law and, for some months in 1776 and 1777, he acted as Chief Justice of the Province.[8]

The Spanish attacked West Florida in 1780, and as a result, that province ceased to be a British possession the following year. East Florida remained loyal to the British Crown throughout the American Revolution and a considerable number of immigrants who did not wish to sever their allegiance to Great Britain took up residence in the province. Even so, East Florida was still sparsely inhabited.

The advent of American Independence would mean that the province was separated from the loyal British possessions in the North by a coast-line of a thousand miles. Rumours swept through the settlers that the mother-country was on the point of ceding the land back to Spain. A petition was drawn up, asking the British Government to retain possession of the province, and The Revd. John Forbes was sent to England to present the appeal in person. But it was too late. On the 30th September 1783 Great Britain signed a Treaty at Versailles providing for the cession of East Florida back to Spain. It had been a British possession for twenty years. After the cession, the Roman Catholic religion alone was tolerated and the church building of St Peter's was demolished. The Spanish occupation lasted until 1821, when East Florida passed into control of the United States of America, and freedom of worship was once more allowed.

John Forbes died shortly after his arrival in Britain in 1783. He was only forty-three years old, but his missionary labours and those of his colleagues in the nineteen years from 1764 to 1783 survived. In 1831, the Domestic and Foreign Missionary Society of the Protestant Episcopal Church – reported "Although the Church was extinct as a visible body, yet some few scattered persons with praiseworthy constancy adhered to the true faith; and, from the circumstances of possessing the Book of Common Prayer, were enabled to worship God in the use of our invaluable Liturgy."[9]

NATIVE AMERICANS

During the eighteenth century, the main focus of Anglican missionary activity with Native Americans was amongst the Iroquois, a powerful combination of the "Five Nations" in the Province of New York. Amongst those five tribes, the Mohawks had a place of primacy, and occupied the easternmost part of the territory. The friendship of the Iroquois was important to the colonists for three very different reasons, the first being defence. The Five Nations were a buffer between them and the French in the North, who then occupied Canada. Then there was a valuable trade in skins and furs, the result of hunting skills of the Iroquois. The third reason (which motivated the Society for the Propagation of the Gospel) was a response to the Dominical command to make disciples of all the nations. The Society concentrated, almost exclusively, on work with the Mohawks. Although the number of clergy was small and the result of their labours outwardly disappointing, yet the Mohawk Mission is worthy of remembrance as an extraordinary piece of heroic Anglican missionary enterprise.

In reviewing The Faithful Mohawks in 1938, an American priest-historian put the mission, into perspective:–

"For more than sixty years there was a succession of devoted, earnest, and industrious missionaries, struggling to instruct and edify the temperamental and ungovernable Iroquois, in spite of the opposition of the Dutch traders, the French Imperialists and the Jesuit diplomats. Our people do not know – and certainly the standard American histories have never told them – that a clergyman named William Andrews worked against fearful odds, a pioneer in a most hostile environment, and that he began the translation of the Book of Common Prayer in the Indian tongue; or that another

Anglican clergyman, John Miln, laboured among those warlike people from 1727 to 1736 and prepared discourses in the Mohawk language, and wore himself out at his task so that he had to return home in order to recuperate. It was The Revd. Henry Barclay, afterwards rector of Trinity Church, New York, who toiled in that precarious situation from 1735 to 1746, and while ministering to the Indians, translated the Communion Service, the orders for Baptism and Matrimony and the Burial of the Dead, and various passages of Scripture, as well as occasional prayers into the native tongue, thus carrying forward the work which Andrews had started. The Revd. John Ogilvie, who followed Barclay and remained among the Indians some twelve years, was an heroic figure. During the contest which resulted in the final surrender of Canada to the English, he served as army chaplain and enjoyed the confidence of such men as Wolfe, Prideaux and Amherst. Thomas Browne and Harry Munro might also get mentioned – hard-working missionaries among the Indians, and John Stuart, who began his ministrations among the New York Indians about four years before the American Revolution and who may be regarded as the father of the Church of Canada, translated St. Mark's gospel into the Mohawk language."[10]

Dr. Legare Pennington might have added two more names to complete the list – those of The Revd.s. "Thorogood" Moore and Thomas Barclay. A glance at the names indicates the Scottish background of virtually every one of the clergy involved.

Thomas Moore 1704-1705
Thomas Barclay 1705-1722
William Andrews 1712-1722
John Miln 1728-1735
Henry Barclay 1737-1747
John Ogilvie 1750-1761
Thomas Browne 1761-1767
Harry Munro 1767-1775
John Stuart 1770-1783

In response to a request from Lord Cornbury, the Governor of New York Province, the SPG sent out the first missionary in 1704. He went to the Mohawk territory at Albany beyond the West Bank of the Hudson River about a hundred and fifty miles from the city of New York. Albany was then a town of some two hundred and fifty houses, protected by a stockaded fort and two companies of soldiers.

After a year he returned to New York and wrote disconsolately: "Tho I have been at Albany a twelvemonth, and have used all the means I could think of in order to get the good will of the Indians that they might accept of me, yet I could never get of them as much as to tell me whether they could or no. Tis from the behaviour of the Christians here", he concluded "that they have had and still have their Notions of

Christianity, which God knows has been and is generally such, that I can't but think has made the Indians even hate Christianity.". Like Andrews and Barclay after him, he complained about the alcohol problems that the colonists had brought with them – "Indeed, the Christians selling the Indians so much rum as they do is a sufficient bar if there were no other, against their embracing Christianity."[11]

Moore went to Burlington for a time, was affronted by the transvestism of Lord Cornbury and spoke out against the Governor, as a result of which he was imprisoned. He escaped, took ship back to Britain, but was lost when the ship foundered. So the first attempt at mission to the Mohawks ended in failure.

The next attempt was by The Revd. Thomas Barclay, a graduate of St Andrews University, who was chaplain to the British garrison at Albany and who undertook a wider remit as a part-time missioner to the Mohawks. He had more success than Moore, and was able to report on baptisms and on meetings of fifty or more, within a year of his appointment in 1709.

He worked on faithfully combining his two responsibilities until what appears to have been a mental breakdown in 1722. The advent of William Andrews in 1712 certainly reduced the pastoral load that he was carrying. (It was, incidentally, Thomas Barclay whose broad Scottish accent gave rise to the complaint by Governor William Burnet. Burnet might have been more sympathetic. He came of Scottish stock himself, his father was the great Gilbert Burnet, bishop of Salisbury, 1689-1715, and the last priest in Scottish orders to become a bishop in the Church of England for two hundred and fifty years).

In 1710, five of the Indian Sachems (chiefs) were persuaded to travel to England. One died on the voyage, but the remaining four were presented to Queen Anne. They expressed a desire for Christian teaching, and the Archbishop of Canterbury (Tenison) commended them to the SPG. The four Sachems came in person to the headquarters of the Society to make their request. Their visit so impressed the Society that it was decided to alter the general policy, and concentrate some of its resources upon the Mohawks. The following resolution was passed:–

"1/ That the design of propagating the Gospel in foreign parts does chiefly and principally relate to the conversion of heathens and infidels: and therefore that branch of it ought to be prosecuted preferably to all others.

2/ That in consequence thereof immediate care be taken to send itinerant missionaries to preach the Gospel amongst the Six Nations of the Indians, according to the primary intention of the late King William of glorious memory.

3/ That a stop be put to the sending of any more missionaries among Christians, except to such places whose ministers are or shall be dead, or removed; and unless it may consist with the funds of the Society to prosecute both designs"

The Society eventually found a missionary in The Revd. William Andrews, a Scottish Episcopalian, who arrived in New York in October 1712. It was a hard life and difficult work. "In the winter season four or five months we can scarce stir abroad by reason of the Extreme Coldness of the Weather and deep Snows, and in the summer tormented with fflyes and muscheetoes and can't stir abroad without being in danger of being stung with the snakes, there are so many of them Especially the Rattlesnakes."[12]

In these difficult circumstances, the heroic Andrews carried on for seven years. He had, at first, met with some success, but the early promise soon faded away. The Indians lacked perseverance, they expected to be bribed with presents, and even if he had wished to, he could not match the French Jesuits in gifts of food and clothing. He had done all that a man could do, and far more than most would have attempted. He resigned in 1798 and died two years later.

HENRY BARCLAY
Missionary to the Mohawks 1737-1747

It was not for another sixteen years that a full-time missoner was appointed. He was young Henry Barclay; the son of the Scottish Episcopalian Chaplain at Albany, who had been a part-time missonary to the Indians, gaining a large number of adherents, and who was succeeded by The Revd. John Miln who worked from Albany until Henry Barclay's appointment. Henry Barclay knew the Indians and something of their language. He went first as a catechist and soon had a school of forty children with evening classes for adults. "The Indians expressed a great love and esteem for him" reported the Commissioner "and they had very much reformed since his working among them". In due course Barclay went to England, was ordained deacon and priest, and returned to take charge at Albany as well as at Fort Hunter. He continued for eleven years until the war with the French, and the consequent devastation of the area made his work impossible. "Albany has become a wilderness, and numbers of People who were possess'd of good Estates are reduced to Poverty". When he was offered the important charge of Trinity Church, New York in October 1746, Barclay accepted and left the Indian Mission, which was once again suspended.[13]

Barclay had picked out as a promising replacement, The Revd. John Ogilvie, who began work at Albany in 1750. During the interval, the work had suffered a great deal. "I find (the Indians) universally degenerated." Ogilvie wrote to the SPG, "since the war they are entirely given up to Drunkenness. Many seem to have lost all sense of religion, and the best are in a State of Indifference". He worked tirelessly for them for the next eleven years, but fighting with the French broke out again, and much of his time was taken up with the pastoral care of the troops. "Besides my duty in the Army", he wrote, "I attend the Indians, and give them Prayers, as often on weekdays as the public service of the Camp will admit, and on Sunday the Gen. always gives public orders for divine service among the Indians".

Ogilvie accompanied the Royal American Regiment to Niagara. The Mohwaks were all in this service, as were members of all the Five Nations.[14]

In Ogilvie's absence on military duty, The Revd. Thomas Browne was sent as Chaplain at Albany, and at the Mohawk Castle. He was not officially appointed as missionary until Ogilvie's Commission as chaplain to one battalion was confirmed. Browne felt that his presence was not the answer to the Society's good intentions, and resigned in 1767. He was replaced by The Revd. Harry Munro in the same year and the Mohawk's work began to revive. In January 1770, Munro was able to report: "Baptised during the last half-year, sixty-eight, one Indian adult. In September last, I preached at Sir William Johnston's; baptised six, and married one couple. I am now again returned from visiting Sir William and the Indians at Fort Hunter, where I preached last Sunday and administered the Sacrament; and am now preparing for another journey to Conojoharec, the Upper Castle being seventy miles from Albany, there to preach and administer the sacrament at the request of some old Indians who are communicants, and who could not attend at Lower Castle."

In the same year, 1770, The Revd. John Stuart was appointed solely to the Mohawk Mission at Fort Hunter. So began a ministry which was to end with him and his Mohawks in Canada. Stuart claimed to be in the direct line of the Royal Family of Scotland. His grandfather had emigrated from Scotland to Ireland. His father had married Mary Dinwiddie from Glasgow and the pair of them had then crossed the Atlantic. Although brought up as a Reformed Presbyterian, John was ordained deacon and priest in the Church of England by the Bishop of London in 1770. He was thirty years old at the time. After ordination, he came back to spend eleven years on the Mohawk Mission. During the war of Independence he suffered considerably. No word was heard from him for some years until he reached safety in 1781. While his Mohawks had taken refuge in Canada, Stuart himself had been kept prisoner at Schenectady. "My house has frequently been broken open by Mobs" he reported to the SPG, "My property plundered, and indeed every kind of indignity offered to my Person by the lowest of the Populace ... My Church was plundered by the Rebels and the Pulpit Cloth taken away from the Pulpit: it was afterward imployed as a Tavern, the Barrel of rum placed on the Reading Desk. The succeeding Season it was used as a stable; and now serves as a Fort to protect a Set of as great Villains as ever disgraced Humanity". Stuart settled in Canada, and went back to ministering to his Mohawks there.[15]

These pioneers left their mark on the Anglican Church. They were the first missionaries to be sponsored by an agency of the Church of England to minister outside the bounds of the European community. Andrews, Miln, Barclay and Stuart had all engaged in translating the scriptures and the Prayer Books into the Mohawk language. They were the forerunners of a long line of apostolic men whose lives adorn the pages of Anglican history.

Chapter VII
THE SOUTHERN COLONIES

THE BACKGROUND

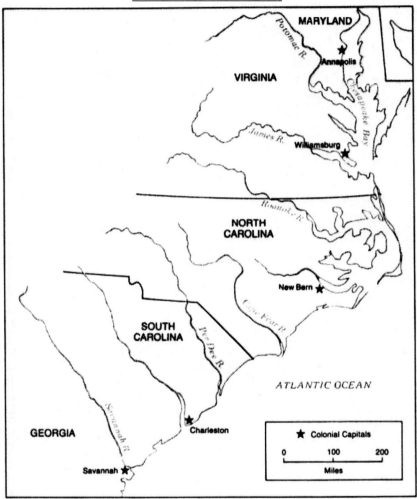

THE SOUTHERN COLONIES

In this and in the two following chapters, there are series of snapshots of the ministry of a few of the many Scottish clergy who served the Church in America during the colonial period.

The clergy arrived from a varied background. A handful of them were already in Scottish or Irish orders. The rest came from two main sources. One was the Society for the Propagation of the Gospel which sent a total of 340 missionaries to the thirteen American colonies. The other source was from locally recruited candidates who were sent to England for ordination, equipped with a Title to Orders.

From the beginning the Society maintained extensive records. These included some personal particulars of the men they sent. They also required from each of them, a regular report on their ministry in the form of a Notitia Parochialis, giving details of numbers, baptisms performed etc. As a result it is possible to build up a picture of many of the SPG missionaries and their work. By contrast, it is often difficult to discover the same things about some of the locally recruited clergy, particularly during the early years. A classic example of this was Alexander Murray who is mentioned below.

During the period from 1701 until 1783, the Southern Colonies received a total of 107 missionaries who came under the auspices of SPG. These were distributed as follows:-

Virginia 2
Maryland 5
North Carolina 33
South Carolina 54
Georgia 13

The reason for the disparity in numbers was due, in part, to the Society's view that Blair and Bray between them had already laid much of the foundation work, including advice to Bishop Compton on sending clergy to Virginia and Maryland. These were the two colonies in which the Scottish element among the clergy had been most evident. It was also in part due to the fact that it was clearly easier to attract men to those colonies where Anglicanism was established, where there existed settled church structures and where there was an assured house and stipend.

Virginia had established the Church of England with a system of parishes and stipends as early as 1612.

Maryland, under the Maryland Charter of 1632, had been granted to Cecil Calvert, Lord Baltimore, a Roman Catholic, as its "Absolute Lord and Proprietor" and under him, Trinitarian Christians were given complete religious freedom – something of a novelty in an age when there was widespread compulsory religious conformity elsewhere. Following the arrival in Britain of William and Mary, Maryland was taken from Baltimore and became a royal colony. When the first royal governor, Lionel Copley, arrived in 1692 he brought with him the customary instructions from the Crown to "take especial care that God be devoutly and duly served, that the Book of Common Prayer be regularly used and the Blessed Sacrament be administered according to the Rites of the Church of England". A series of Acts beginning in 1692 initiated the process of establishment for the Anglican Church, dividing the colony into parishes (thirty to begin with) and providing for a tithe of forty pounds of tobacco to pay for the building of churches, and thereafter to be used for the payment of stipends.

In South Carolina, an Act was passed in 1706 providing £330 apiece for building eight churches, and for clergy stipends to be paid out of public funds.

In North Carolina, an Act was passed in 1715 providing for nine parishes, and a stipend of £50 per annum for each priest.

Georgia, which did not become the thirteenth colony until 1732, had full religious toleration, and provision for the ministry of the Church of England.

VIRGINIA[1]

The name of one Scottish priest that will always be associated with Virginia is that of Comissary James Blair, whose American ministry is recounted in Chapter V. But Blair was only one of many Scots who served in the colony. They were not always universally popular.

The complaint of Governor Edmond Andros to the Archbishop of Canterbury in 1697 that Blair "was filling the country with Scottish clergy" had been given short shrift. So, too, was that of the Huguenot minister, Nicholas Moreau, who declared that most of the Virginia clergy were "Scotchmen, people barely educated, whose lives are more fitted to make heathens than Christians", a charge which echoed exactly that of Andros, with whose party Moreau was aligned.

In 1764, The Revd. Isaac William Gilberne, Minister of Lunenburg Church in Richmond County, wrote to the Bishop of London criticising the willingness of some laymen to give Titles to Orders to young men seeking ordination, without properly investigating their characters or their qualifications. He went on to say that "above three-fourths of the clergy here, I am told, are from Scotland, many of whom came out as indentured servants, schoolmasters etc."

This was partly true. Some of the clergy had arrived in America as schoolmasters or tutors to private families. Many of them though, proved to be the best and most active priests in the Church. Then, too, although there were many Scots who occupied parishes, they certainly did not make up the three-fourths of the clergy that Gilberne claimed.

A more accurate assessment than Gilberne's may be gauged from figures cited in a recent history of the American Church by Professor David Holmes of the College of William and Mary. Of the 174 clergy who served in Virginia from 1723 until the Revolution, no less than 46 were graduates from Scottish Universities, 45 came from William and Mary, 1 from Yale and 59 from Oxford and Cambridge.

SOME OF THE SCOTTISH CLERGY
Alexander Murray and Robert Rose

Alexander Murray (or Moray) and Robert Rose appear in a fasinating history, in a later chapter, in connection with the struggle for an American episcopate. It is known that he was an ardent supporter of the Stuart cause, who went into exile to Virginia in 1652 after the defeat of Charles I at the battle at Worcester. He was appointed minister of Ware Parish in Gloucester County where he remained until his death. Sadly no parish records exist to tell more of his service there. Robert Rose was regarded as one of the most outstanding of the Anglican Clergy in the colonial period of Virginia. He was born in Inverness-shire in 1704, and died at Richmond, Virginia in 1751. Ordained and licensed (for Virginia parishes, he became minister of Saint Anne's Parish, Essex County, at the age of twenty-one. He remained there until his appointment in 1744 as Rector of Saint Anne's Parish in Albemarle County which he held until his death. Whilst in Saint Anne's, Albemarle, Rose kept a daily diary of his activities from January 1746 until 1751 which gives a clear picture of an energetic colonial priest carrying out his ministerial duties.This in itself would have fully occupied most men, but the diary shows that he had developed other areas of skill, in medicine, surveying and in land speculation. The Inventory of his estate at the time of his death showed that he had acquired several thousand acres of plantation as well as lots in various towns throughout the colony. The Inventory also listed a hundred and one slaves on his properties. His epitaph in Richmond speaks of "his extraordinary genius and capacity in all the polite and useful areas of life, though equalled by few, were yet exceeded by the great goodness of his heart."

Charles Rose

Robert Rose was not the only member of his family to serve as a priest in Virginia. His younger brother, Charles, also crossed the Atlantic ten years later, and became minister of Yeocomico Parish in Westmoreland County in 1736, remaining there until his death in 1761.

Robert Innes

A kinsman of the Roses', Robert Innes, was born in Western Alves, Inverness-shire (where Robert Rose was born in 1720). Innes was ordained and licensed for overseas service in July 1748. Later that year he became minister of Drysdale Parish in Caroline County, where he served for seventeen years until his death in 1765.

David and William Stuart

Another family which provided clergy for Virginia was that of David Stuart who left Scotland in 1715 to become minister of St. Paul's Church, King George County. He was succeeded some thirty-five years later by his son, William. Together, the two Stuarts served St. Paul's for nearly eighty years. During William's incumbency a new church was built. "This saintly man left a name that shines almost with a halo in the records that follow him. His goodness and eloquence and lovable personality appear to have strengthened and beautified the spirit of the parish and led it into great religious prosperity."

William Stuart continued his ministry for almost forty years until increasing infirmity compelled him to resign. His letter of resignation is an indication of his concern as a faithful priest for the welfare of his flock.

"To the Vestry of St. Paul's Parish

Gentlemen, I have been curate of this parish upward of forty years. My own conscience bears me witness, and I trust my parishioners (though many of them have fallen asleep) will also witness, that until age and infirmities disabled me, I always, so far as my infirmities would allow, faithfully discharged my duties as a minister of the Gospel. It has given me many hours of anxious conern that the services of the Church should be so long discontinued on my account. The spirit indeed is willing, but the flesh is weak. I therefore entreat the favour of you to provide me a sucessor as soon as you can, that divine service be discontinued no longer, and at the end of the year the glebe shall be given up to him by your affectionate servant, WILLIAM STUART"

William Wylie (or Willie)

William Wylie had emigrated to Virginia from the Scottish Highlands as a young man. Believing himself to be called to ordination, he approached the Commissary, William Dawson, who had succeeded James Blair in 1734.

Dawson approved of the young man's character and educational qualifications, but declined to recommend him to the Bishop of London on the grounds that there was no vacant parish at the time to which Wylie could be appointed. It says much for the determination and sense of vocation of this young Scot that he went to England at his own expense. The Bishop of London was satisfied as to Wylie's fitness, and duly ordained him as deacon and priest. However, he was unable to issue him with a Licence because he had not received the necessary recommendation from the Commissary, nor could he receive the King's Bounty.

Wylie returned to Virginia and was appointed Minister of Albemarle parish in Sussex County where he remained until his death in 1776. He was appointed to serve as acting Commissary in 1771.

MARYLAND[2]

As in Virginia, most of the clergy who served in Maryland during the colonial period came either from local recruitment or by direct immigration from Britain. Only five men were sent out by the Society for the Propagation of the Gospel. Like the Virginian clergy, too, a sizeable proportion were Scotsmen or of Scots descent. For example, one of the first of the original thirty parishes (All Faiths', Saint Mary's County) was served by five rectors between 1703 and the Revolution, and three of these were Scots.

It was not that Scots clergy were universally popular. An anonymous publication of 1722 entitled Character of the Clergy of Maryland gave a list of twenty-two clergymen with their parishes and a statement of character after each name. It is apparent that the politics and country of origin had much to do with the character assessments. Whigs were almost invariably amongst "the best of men and true Christians". Scots, on the other hand, were variously described as "a grand Tory", "a Rake", "an idiot", "a Tory who belongs to the Society" and so on. Happily, none of this seems to have been borne out by the devoted service that these clergy gave to their charges.

All Faiths Parish, Saint Mary's County. The three Scots incumbents referred to above were:-

> Robert Scott 1709-1733 died 1733
> John Urquhart 1733-1764 died 1764
> John Stephen 1767-1786 died 1786

They served altogether for sixty-eight years, died in office, and spent their entire ministries in the one parish.

John Lang

John Lang was a Scottish priest who had served briefly in Virginia before spending his ministry in Maryland. Ordained in London in 1725, his initial appointment was to Saint Peter's Parish in New Kent County, Virginia. There is a long letter from him preserved in the Scottish Record Office in Edinburgh. It was addressed to the unknown peer who had recommended him for ordination and preferment in Virginia.

He had begun his ministry with considerable social advantages, bearing as he did recommendations also from the Earl of Orkney and from the Bishops of London and of Norwich. The Governor offered him the choice of any vacant parish in the colony. Saint Peter's was judged to be "one of the very best (parishes) in the colony, with a salary of 16,000 pounds of sweet scented tobacco". Moreover, "the people were of the best sort, abundantly civil and courteous, although the Common rank be very ignorant, opinionative and unmannerly".

However, Lang became very concerned with the moral tone of Virginia, and believed that "a Spiritual Jurisdiction" should be created "for the Suppression of Vice even in the Clergy as well as the Laity". In fact, there had been no "Spiritual Jurisdiction" in the form of a Commissary since the death of Henry Compton, Bishop of London, in 1713. Lang went on to imply that the previous Commissary, James Blair, had been too soft on crime and the causes of crime. Although Lang himself had only been in Holy Orders for less than two years, he offered himself for the office of Commissary.

He also wrote to the Bishop of London about the moral state of the colony. However Blair was re-appointed and a disappointed Lang moved to Maryland after only two years at Saint Peter's. On five occasions he wrote to ask for a parish in England.. In this, too, he was disappointed. He spent the rest of his life in Saint Luke's Parish in Queen Anne's County from 1728 to 1734, and then in Saint James' Parish, Anne Arundel, from 1734 until his death at Saint James' in 1748.

David Lowe

Lowe received the King's Bounty for service in Maryland in April 1764, and was appointed to serve in All Hallow's Parish in Anne Arundel County. He arrived in 1765 after ordination by the Archbishop of Canterbury on the recommendation of Lord Baltimore. The Governor of Maryland, Horatio Sharpe, was impressed by Lowe's appearance, but not, apparently, by his strong Scottish accent. Sharpe wrote "I wish he may preach as well as he looks, and pronounce English a little better than the generality of our Scotch Clergymen."

Lowe continued to serve in All Hallows' until 1776, when his loyalist convictions prevented him from taking the prescribed oath of allegiance. He was permitted to leave Maryland on condition that he did not "return to this State … without the leave of the Governor and Council".

James Wilkinson

Wilkinson arrived in Shrewsbury Parish, Kent County in 1713, moving on to All Saints' Parish, Calvert County in 1722. He remained at All Saints' until 1767, one of the longest incumbencies of any of the colonial clergy. He was the priest described in the anonymous 1722 publication as "an idiot and a Tory". Wilkinson's long and faithful service at All Saints' belies the accusation that he was "an idiot". He was certainly a Tory but that did not detract from the effectiveness of his ministry.

His successor at All Saints' was Thomas John Claggett, who was destined to be the first American to be consecrated on American soil to become the first Bishop of Maryland.

John Gordon

Not all Scots Clergy were Tories. One of the most outstanding colonial rectors was John Gordon who served as Incumbent of Saint Michael's Parish, Talbot County, for the forty-one years from 1749 to 1790.

Born in Aberdeen in 1717, he graduated from Queens College, Oxford and was ordained in 1745. His first appointment was to Saint Anne's Church, Annapolis from where he went to Saint Michael's four years later.

Gordon was an ardent Whig and shortly after his arrival in Annapolis preached against the Young Pretender's rebellion aimed at restoring the Stuarts to the throne.

His Whig principles allowed him to embrace American Independence and to continue as rector of Saint Michael's. He remained unmarried until the age of forty. It was then that the Vestry, under an Act of the Assembly, placed an annual levy of three hundred pounds of tobacco on bachelors in Saint Michael's Parish. Gordon then found a wife. He continued his ministry until his death at the age of seventy-three in 1790.

THE CAROLINAS AND GEORGIA

By contrast with Virginia and Maryland, the other three Southern Colonies – North Carolina, South Carolina and Georgia – had many fewer Anglicans. This was in spite of the assistance of the Society who had sent one hundred missionaries altogether to the area. The number is somewhat deceptive, since many of the clergy served for only one or two years, some of them dying from "a flux", "a fever" or an "inward heat".

In North Carolina there had been only one clergyman in 1701. By 1765 the number had increased to five. By the end of the Revolution there were only eleven left in their parishes.

South Carolina began the century with two clergy and was left with eighteen by 1783. Georgia had no clergy to start with and at the most had only ever had five Anglican churches.

SOME OF THE SCOTS

The Gardens

The most outstanding Scottish priest to minister in the Southern Colonies was The Revd. Alexander Garden whose name appears in Chapter IV above. He served in South Carolina for thirty-five years from 1719 until 1754. For twenty-six of those years he held the office of Commissary for the Bishop of London. His entire ministry was spent in Saint Philip's, Charles Town.

Garden was followed in the service of the church in South Carolina by his nephew, also Alexander. Ordained deacon and priest by the Bishop of Gloucester in 1743, he was accepted by the Society for the Propagation of the Gospel and ministered in Saint Thomas's for the next twenty-one years.

Robert Cuming

One of the clergy with the shortest length of ministry was Robert Cuming, a Scottish graduate ordained in 1748. He went straight out to serve in Saint John's, South Carolina, but died the year following his arrival in the Colony.

John Boyd

Another comparatively short ministry was that of John Boyd, a graduate of the University of Glasgow. He had formerly practised as a physician in Virginia. In 1732 he travelled to England to be ordained, returning to Bertie Parish, Albemarle, North Carolina to serve as an SPG missionary there. His nominal parish was a hundred miles long by fifty miles wide, but in fact he was the only Anglican priest in the whole colony for a time. Not surprisingly, the Society designated him as an Itinerant Minister. He regularly preached in seven different places, and rode several hundred miles in a month.

In 1735 he reported that he had baptised a thousand children and thirty adults. Sadly, his ministry was cut short by his death in 1738, only six years after he had accepted the challenge of this most demanding assignment.

The Wesleys and Whitefield[3]

No account of Anglicanism in the Southern Colonies can fail to mention, if only briefly, the ministry of The Revd. John Wesley in Georgia.

Sent out by the SPG in 1735 he spent only two years in the Colony, but during that time he managed to publish his first hymnal. His brother Charles, who accompanied him, spent only one year in Georgia acting as Secretary to the Governor, James Oglethorpe.

Indifference to his ministry on the part of the colonists and the native Americans was added to his quarrels with local authorities provoked by his autocratic manner and methods. This persuaded him to return to England, although his departure was precipitated by the need to avoid a libel action founded on his repelling from Holy Communion a Mrs Williamson, who (as Miss Hopkey) had rejected Wesley's offer of marriage a short time before.

A year after his return to England he experienced his conversion at a meeting with Moravians in Fetter Lane Chapel, London. It was from that point that he began his prototype pattern of Methodist meetings. It is interesting to remember that both brothers still remained as priests in the Church of England at the time of their deaths.

The ship taking John Wesley back to England crossed with that carrying his successor, George Whitefield, out to Georgia. Unlike Wesley who was, at the time of his ministry in the colony, a convinced High Churchman, Whitefield was an ardent Evangelical. His disregard for the Prayer Book brought him into conflict with Commissary Garden, who felt compelled to suspend him. The practical effect of this was not great, as Whitefield went on a number of extended preaching tours throughout the colonies, sparking off what became known as the Great Awakening. It was a Revivalist Movement that had much more effect outside Anglicanism, at any rate in the early days. But it did become extremely influential in changing the course of American Protestantism.

"Thirdly, *With respect to the Society.*

"I. THAT each of them keep a constant and regular Correspondence with the Society, by their Secretary.
"II. That they send every six Months an Account of the State of their respective Parishes, according to the Scheme annexed, No. II.
"III. That they communicate what shall be done at the Meetings of the Clergy, when settled, and whatsoever else may concern the Society."

N° I.

Notitia Parochialis; to be made by each Minister soon after his Acquaintance with his People, and kept by him for his own Ease and Comfort, as well as the Benefit of his Parishioners.

I.	II.	III.	IV.	V.	VI.	VII.
Names of Parishioners	Profession of Religion	Which of them baptized	When baptized	Which of them Communicants	When they first communicated	What Obstructions they meet with in their Ministration

N° II.

Notitia Parochialis; or an Account to be sent Home every six Months to the Society by each Minister, concerning the spiritual State of their respective Parishes.

I. *Number of Inhabitants.*	
II. *No. of the Baptized.*	
III. *No. of Adult Persons baptized this Half-year.*	
IV. *No. of actual Communicants of the* Church of England.	
V. *No. of those who profess themselves of the* Church of England.	
VI. *No. of Dissenters of all Sorts, particularly Papists.*	
VII. *No. of Heathens and Infidels.*	
•VIII. *No. of Converts from a prophane, disorderly and unchristian Course, to a Life of Christian Purity, Meekness, and Charity.*	

Chapter VIII
THE MIDDLE COLONIES

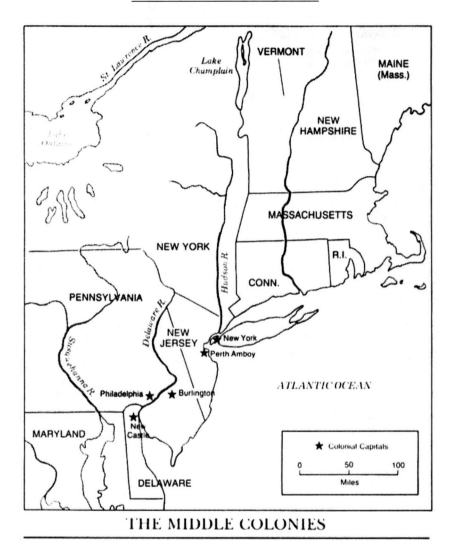

THE MIDDLE COLONIES

The Middle Colonies of New York, New Jersey, Pennsylvania and Delaware received a total of one hundred and forty-nine clergy from the Society for the Propagation of the Gospel. There were, of course, others who came from different sources, but they were a minority. For example, New Jersey could claim the services of forty-seven priests altogether during the Colonial period, and of these, forty-four were SPG men.

Scotland produced a sizeable proportion of the missionary body, and many of these made a major contribution to the life of the four colonies.

Reference has already been made in Chapter V to the pioneers who laboured so heroically in ministering to the native Americans – Stuart, Ogilvie, Andrews, the Barclays' and Browne. There was, too, the first missionary of the Society, Patrick Gordon, who died so tragically within days of his arrival in America.

John Sharpe

One early Scottish priest to serve in New York was The Revd. John Sharpe, born at Bourty in the presbytery of Garioch in 1680. He matriculated in the University of Edinburgh in 1694, and subsequently graduated MA from Aberdeen. He was ordained in 1701 by Henry Compton, Bishop of London, and in July of that year embarked on HMS Southampton intended for service in Maryland. In the event he arrived in Virginia and went thence to New Jersey, where he became a close friend of John Talbot. The pair of them travelled extensively, Sharpe proving himself an able disputant with the Quakers. After Talbot had declined the tempting offer by Governor Cornbury of £130 to become chaplain to the Fort and military forces in New York, Sharpe accepted the post, much to Talbot's regret. "I was loth to part with my good Friend and Companion in Travel" the latter wrote to George Keith. Sharpe continued his ministry in New York for another thirteen years. In 1705 he joined Talbot and other priests in petitioning for the appointment of a bishop to the Colonies. King's College, Aberdeen awarded him a doctorate of Divinity in 1714. Sharpe's great design was to found a free library in New York and his plans for this are in Lambeth Palace Library, together with a catalogue of books belonging to Sharpe "intended to be given as a foundation of a publick library at New York." He returned to London in 1717.

Samuel Auchmuty

Another distinguished priest of Scottish descent to work in New York was The Revd. Samuel Auchmuty. His father was a Scottish lawyer who had become a judge in Boston. Samuel was born in 1722 and graduated from Harvard. He was ordained to the priesthood by the Bishop of London in 1747 and the following year petitioned the SPG for the position of catechist in New York.

Initially, Auchmuty had a class of twenty slave children whom he taught in the evenings. Three years later he reviewed his work in a report:-

"Besides catechising the blacks, I have attending at the same time a number of white children, seldom less than sixty or seventy, which with my black catechumens make up a congregation of one hundred and thirty, sometimes more … Since the second of October 1750, (the date of my letter in the last abstracts) to the second of October

1751, I have baptised sixteen black adults, all well instructed in the principles of our most Holy Religion and constant attendants on Divine Service and catechising. Also thirty-nine black infants".

SAMUEL AUCHMUTY
Rector of Trinity Church, New York 1769-1777

Auchmuty continued and the numbers grew. It was obvious that he was destined for clerical advancement, and in August 1764, he was appointed rector of Trinity Church, New York, the largest and most important charge in the colony, continuing there until his death. He succeeded that other Scot, Henry Barclay.

He was made a Doctor of Divinity of Oxford University in 1766 and of King's (Colombia University) in 1767. A High Churchman and a Loyalist, he was a staunch campaigner for an American episcopate. He suffered considerably for his political beliefs. A letter addressed to him at the beginning of the War of Independence speaks volumes about his stance.

"I am very sorry to find you such an enemy of the Congresses, to Hancock, Adams and their followers." "Whatever you may think of them, Sir, the Wise and Virtuous now applaud their conducts. "We have lately been plagued with a rascally Whig mob" is hardly a decent expression for a Clergyman to use, and your Reflection on our worthy Magistrates is exceedingly illiberal. I would recommend you to avoid party Spirit and Party Prejudice." Auchmuty paid dearly for his political views. In 1776 he had gone on sick leave to New Brunswick. From there he was able to escape with some difficulty, but his wife and daughter were taken by the rebels. In the meantime, the city of New York had been devastated by a disastrous fire. The loss of Trinity Church and his anxiety for the safety of his family proved a terrible blow to him, from which he never recovered. In a letter to the SPG (the last he ever sent) written three weeks after the fire, he said:-

"Upon my arrival at this once delightful City, but now unhappy one, I found everything in great confusion. Upon searching the Rubbish of my late venerable Church and my large elegant house, I could only find a very few trifles of no value except the Church Plate and my own. As Providence has preserved the two Chapels (St. Paul's and St George's), I begin to have divine Service again regularly carried on, after a suspension of nearly three months, and my People begin to flock in so that they soon be filled. The several Churches in this and in the Neighbouring Governments (i.e. Provinces) are converted to the worst of Purposes, and the Society's missionaries by this time are either in a Jail or sent away back into the Country."

"My poor wife and daughters are still in the hands of the Rebels, and God only knows when I shall be able to obtain their Freedom."

All the same, Auchmuty struggled on, hoping against hope for better things to come and ministering to his people to the last, until worn out from the privation which he had suffered, he entered into his rest on the 4 March 1777. He was fifty-five years old.

Charles Inglis

Dr. Auchmuty was succeeded by The Revd. Charles Inglis who had been his assistant at Trinity Church, New York since 1765. Inglis, although born in Ireland, was descended from a noted Scottish clerical family, his immediate forebears for four generations having been priests of the Episcopal Church. His great-great-grandfather had been Rector of Douglas in Lanarkshire. His great-grandfather and grandfather had ministered in Glasgow. The former had been one of the clergy "rabbled" from his living in 1688. Charles Inglis emigrated to Canada in 1755 and after three years as a schoolmaster returned to Britain to be ordained deacon and priest by Zachariah Pearce, the Bishop of Rochester, acting for the Bishop of London. One of his sponsors for ordination was William Smith, Provost of the College of Philadelphia.

Inglis returned to the Anglican mission at Dover, Delaware, where he spent six years before moving to the assistantship of Trinity, New York. He took a considerable interest in the native American missions and wrote a number of letters and papers to SPG and others with plans and schemes for the support and evangelisation of the Mohawks. Temperamentally he was described as "a quiet student and scholar who loved to spend his scanty leisure in literary and intellectual pursuits." Oxford University recognised his merits with the degree of Doctor of Divinity in 1778.

His succession to Dr. Auchmuty could hardly have come at a less propitious time, with Trinity church destroyed and the war raging around him, in which he was known to be firmly on the losing side. In the summer of 1783 he wrote to the SPG "that almost all the loyalists, and among others, himself, will be obliged to fly (for) in the estimation of the new Rulers he labours under an heavy load of guilt."

In November 1783, Inglis resigned from Trinity. Three weeks later he embarked in the convoy of crowded transports with the British troops, and arrived back in London in January 1784. He was to remain in Britain for three and a half years before being consecrated in Lambeth Palace Chapel as the first colonial bishop. He was Bishop of Nova Scotia from August 1787 until his death in 1816 at the age of 82.

Eneas Mackenzie

An earlier New York ministry was that of Eneas Mackenzie. Born about 1675, he was a graduate of Aberdeen and of Edinburgh and had served as Chaplain to the Earl of Cromar before crossing the Atlantic in 1705. Under the auspices of the SPG he ministered in Staten Island at the southern tip of New York for the next seventeen years. It was a faithful and exemplary parish ministry.

Most of the inhabitants of Staten Island were Dutch and French, and the English consisted chiefly of Quakers and Anabaptists. He was permitted to use the French church building until an English church was built. In 1713, the church members in Richmond County returned their thanks to the SPG for the ministry of Mr. Mackenzie, saying that "the most implacable adversaries of our church profess a personal respect for him and joyne with us in giving him the best of characters. His unblameable life affording no occasion of disarrangement to his function, nor discredit to his doctrine. Upon his first introduction to this place, there were not above four or five in the whole country that ever knew anything of our Excellent Liturgy and form of worship, and many knew little more of Religion than the common notion of a Deity, and as the ignorance was great and gross, so was their practice irregular and barbarous. But now, by the blessing of God attending his labours, our church increases, a considerable reformation is wrought and something of the face of Christianity is seen amongst us." Similar thanks were sent by the High Sheriff, Commander-in-Chief and Justice for the establishment of schools under the charge of Mr. Mackenzie.

NEW JERSEY[2]

Of the forty-seven clergy who served in New Jersey in the colonial period, no fewer than thirteen were Scots. There were two further interesting connections between Scotland and New Jersey from this time.

The first was Samuel Seabury. Although he has almost always been identified with New York and Connecticut, he had, in fact begun his ministry in New Jersey where he spent ten years as missionary at New London and Groton.

The other was that of George Keith, whose wife came from a family that pioneered in the Scottish settlement of New Jersey. Keith joined in the imigration with her and became surveyor of the colony. This was during his time as a Quaker, and his preaching tours familiarised him with the area, a splendid preparation for the work he was later to undertake for the Society for Propagating the Gospel.

The following vignettes give an indication of the kind of contribution that New Jersey's Scottish priests made to the infant church there.

Alexander Innes

The first missionary to New Jersey was Alexander Innes, a native of Aberdeenshire and an alumnus of Marischal College. He joined the Scottish emigration to New Jersey arriving sometime in 1685. The following year he was commissioned as a chaplain to the troops at New York, and swore allegiance to King James II. In 1688 the "Glorious Revolution" brought William III and Mary II to the throne. Innes was accused of being a "papist" and an enemy of the new sovereigns.

He found it expedient to leave New York in 1689, and went to live amongst his fellow Scots in New Jersey, where he purchased a farm. From then onwards he acted as a non-stipendiary priest. Even when ill-health compelled him to give up his farm, he continued to minister until his death in 1713.

He wrote legal documents for his neighbours, baptised their children and performed marriages and funerals. He had a wide reputation for his gentility and kindness.

When George Keith came to Middletown in Monmouth County, he stayed at Innes' house and paid him this tribute:- "Mr Innes, being in priest's orders often preached among them, and by preaching and conferences frequently with the Quakers and other sorts of people, as also by his pious conversation has done much good among them and has been very instrumental to bring them over to the Church."

John Talbot, who was one of the architects of mission along with George Keith, hoped that the SPG would engage Innes, because he said, "tis pity these hands

should be put to dig that are fit to cultivate the vineyard."
It would be difficult to overestimate the enormous influence that this good and pious priest had exercised in New Jersey.

John Forbes

Alexander Innes died in 1713. The people of Monmouth County had to wait another twenty years before an Anglican priest came to live amongst them. He was John Forbes, another Scot, who was recruited by the SPG and in 1733 awarded the Royal Bounty to serve in New Jersey.

He was the first official missionary of the Society and, like Innes, ministered amongst his fellow Scots at Christ Church, Middletown.

Forbes has been described as "a diligent, earnest and devoted pastor, a man of excellent spirit" who won many for the Church, expecially amongst his countrymen.

Sadly, he died after only three years in New Jersey. It was a crushing blow for the people who had waited so long for a regular pastor. He died in the autumn of 1736. Another decade elapsed before Forbes' successor arrived.

John Preston

Preston was one of the most interesting of the Scottish clergy who served in the colony of New Jersey. He was born in 1718, the son of Sir George Preston of Edinburgh, a baronet. After graduating from Balliol College, Oxford, he took holy orders and in 1741 was commissioned as chaplain to the British 26th Regiment, in which he spent almost the whole of his ministry.

The Regiment was posted to Perth Amboy in New Jersey in 1767. The resident priest there was dying of tuberculosis, and the Vestry asked Preston if he would stand in, in place of the dying priest-physician.

Preston agreed, and when the Rector (Robert McKean) died the Vestry invited the army chaplain to become their pastor. They confidently asserted that "not a person of the Congregation But will be pleased with his Appointment."

Preston was willing to accept the appointment, provided that it had the approval of his general. The general did approve, and agreed that the chaplain could keep his military appointment and pay to supplement the inadequate parish income of Perth Amboy.

His ministry prospered and he preached to full churches. In addition, the Vestry were content to allow the soldiers of the 26th Regiment to use the church for worship. The Revolution saw the town occupied alternately by British and American troops. In 1777, Preston was compelled to close the church down, and he resumed his regular duties as an army chaplain. He died on duty in March 1781.

George Panton

A late Scottish addition to the New Jersey clergy was The Revd. George Panton, a native of Fraserburgh who went to America in 1771 as a private tutor. In 1773, he was appointed Rector of St. Michael's Church, Trenton in New Jersey.

He aligned himself with the loyalists, and in May 1775 drew up a declaration of loyalty to the Crown which was presented to the House of Assembly for New Jersey. After serving as chaplain to the Prince of Wales's Volunteers, he joined in the general loyalist migration to Upper Canada.

In the meantime, had had ministered at Phillipsburg (Yonkers) New York from December 1777. He returned to Edinburgh in 1785 where his mother was seriously ill, eventually retiring to Kelso where he died in 1811.

His sister, Kathrein, was a friend and parishioner of Alexander Jolly, who held the see of Moray from 1798 to 1838, combining the bishopric with the incumbency of Fraserburgh in Aberdeenshire. When Kathrein died she left a sum of money to erect and endow "a Seminary of Learning or Theological Institution for the education of young men desirous to serve in the Sacred Ministry of the Scotch Episcopal Church". The result of her benefaction was the creation of Edinburgh Theological College.

PENNSYLVANIA AND DELAWARE[3]

Forty-seven of the Society's missionaries found their way to Pennsylvania and Delaware during the Colonial period.

George Ross

The first Mission in Delaware was organised in New Castle in 1704. The Revd. George Ross was sent by the SPG to supply it.

He was born in Balblair, Ross-shire in the North of Scotland in 1679, and graduated Master of Arts from Edinburgh University in 1700. He took up his duties in 1705 and settled down to a devoted ministry in the colony for almost thirty years. He returned to Britain on leave in 1710, and on his return journey fell into the hands of the French by whom he "was carryed prisoner into France".

In March of that year he wrote:- "I as well as others was stript of all my cloaths from the crown of my head to the sole of my foot; in a word, I was left as naked as I was born and that by means of the greedy priest who was Chaplain of the Ship; he perceived that my cloaths were better than his own and therefore he never ceased to importune his Captain till he got leave to change, forsooth with me, so that I am now cloathed in raggs, in testimony of my bondage".

On his release, he returned to Pennsylvania to the Mission at Chester. There, he reported, Quakerism had "taken deep root" and was "cultivated by art and policy and recommended by fashion and interest, so that the doctrines of Christ met with much reproach and opposition."
It was a hard field to cultivate. Nevertheless, both there and again at New Castle the Church graduallly gained in strength.
Ross continued as a missionary of the SPG until his death in 1734 at the age of fifty-five.

Aeneas Ross

George Ross's son, Aeneas, entered the service of the Society in 1741 and continued to serve in Pennsylvania until his death in 1782.
On his appointment, he went to Philadelphia to one of the most important parishes in the colony. He went from there to Oxford and thence to New Castle where his father had ministered before him in the years 1705-1708 and again from 1713 until 1734.
A year after his arrival in Philadelphia, he wrote to the Society:-
"Since my first coming here, I have baptiz'd upward of 100 persons, 18 of whom were adults, 12 were Negroes, men and women, who appear'd publickly before the Congregation and were examin'd in, and said their Catechisms to the Admiration of All that heard them. Nine of them I baptiz'd together the 17th Janry last, the like sight never before seen in Philad'a Church."
It was a pattern of apostolic ministry that Ross was to continue throughout his service.

William Smith

The foundation of the College of William and Mary in Williamsburg, Virginia by James Blair has already been referred to. That educational institution has continued to flourish for three hundred years. Another Scottish priest very much involved in the American academic world was William Smith. Born in Aberdeen in 1727, he graduated Master of Arts in King's College there in 1747, when he moved to London to work for the Society for the Propagation of the Gospel. Four years later he sailed for New York to become a private tutor for a couple of years during which time he published A General Idea of the College of Mirania. This outlined the kind of institution he thought would best suit the needs and circumstances of a new country. History, agriculture and religion were strongly emphasised and the college would take under its wing a school for training men destined for "the mechanic profession". He returned to England in 1753 and was made deacon and priest in December of that year, one of his fellow ordinands being Samuel Seabury, the future bishop. Whilst in Britain, Smith obtained a copy of the new regulations for King's College, Aberdeen, some of the principles of which he incorporated in proposals for the Academy and Charitable School, Philadelphia, where he began teaching in 1754.

From that time until the Revolution, he was the dominant influence as Provost in the affairs of the Academy, which became a degree granting College in 1755. Like Blair, he was a man of great energy, and played a leading part, too, in the affairs of Pennsylvania as well as developing the College. He was a consistent advocate of securing the Episcopate for America, and was widely believed to have hoped to be appointed himself. His academic work was recognised by the Universities of Oxford, King's College, Aberdeen and Dublin, all of which conferred upon him the honorary degree of Doctor of Divinity. The College became the University of Pennsylvania in 1791 and Smith was its first Provost.

He was the chairman of the committee appointed in 1785 to adapt the Prayer Book to American conditions and did much of the work himself. He was largely instrumental in gaining approval for the adoption of the Scottish Liturgy as substantially the eucharistic office for the American Church, which had been part of Seabury's concordat with the Scottish bishops a year before. Despite his honours and responsibilities, he never enjoyed the greatest respect from his contemporaries, one of whom wrote of him: "Unhappily his conduct in all his relations and situations was opposed to his talents and profession … he early contracted a love for strong drink and became towards the close of his life an habitual drunkard … His temper was irritable, and when angry he swore in the most extravagant manner. With all his faults, however, he was one of the ablest, most versatile, and most influential Pennsylvanians of his day. He possessed genius, taste and learning. The importance of his service for practically a quarter of a century during the formative years of what is now the University of Pennsylvania is incalculable, and his contribution to education in general not inconsiderable."

William Lindsay

Not every Scottish priest proved to be an asset to America or a good advertisement for Scotland. A few got into trouble for their political stance, and this became increasingly the case as Independence approached. The case of Samuel Auchmuty was one in point.

Perhaps the worst example was William Lindsay. He graduated MA from the University of Glasgow in 1723. With a number of relatives and friends he visited America where he was encouraged to seek ordination. He returned to Britain in 1724, was duly ordained and accepted by the SPG, receiving the King's Bounty for Pennsylvania. He settled in Bristol in that Colony in 1725, ostensibly to exercise an itinerant ministry that included part of New Jersey. It soon became apparent that

Lindsay was a priest who would have been eminently qualified for inclusion in any provincial Clergy Caution List. A New Jersey historian, Dr. Nelson Burr, listed the crimes and misdemeanours of this renegade clergyman.

"The Society at first lent a sympathetic ear to Lindsay's repeated complaints of heavy travelling expenses, worn-out clothing, almost constant illness, dangerous ferries, pressing debts, and the necessity of helping his aged and poor parents in Ireland. He successfully requested a gratuity, having excited compassion by his melancholy pleas, and hints that he would soon be near death. He stressed his devotion to the church in Bristol, which he claimed to have found in "a very mean Condition" declaring that he had repaired the glebe house at his own expense, and that he lived peaceably with the people, even though they subscribed nothing to support him.

But in 1744 the Society was rudely shocked by learning "very base, mean and Scandalous things" against him, reported to a clerical meeting in Philadelphia. Colin Campbell, who vowed that he had no personal grudge against Lindsay, informed the Society of the charges, sustained by sworn affidavits from several persons. He had demanded a high fee for baptizing a poor woman convert from Quakerism in Burlington. He had sold the Society's Bibles and other books sent him to distribute to the poor, and had got a church Bible and Prayer Book for Trenton under false pretenses. He had even defrauded the prisoners in jail there, of a collection made for them in the courthouse at Christmas. He had offended many Churchmen by lodging in a Quaker's house for three or four years and had lied to the Society in 1738 by complaining of hardships and fatigue, to get a gratuity, when he was in good health. He had extorted money for publishing banns of marriage, neglected places in his mission for five years at a time, and taken the parish library at Bristol. He was an habitual drunkard, and had been so soused at a marriage in 1743 that he fell from his horse. He had even attempted to debauch women on the public road. Campbell declared that sectarians had increased in the mission because of Lindsay's bad behaviour. He was doing "more harm than the pious labours of six or more worthy missionarys can do good, and had "much sowered" the temper of the people at Trenton."

Colin Campbell was a fellow-Scot who served in both Pennsylvania and New Jersey. Lindsay denied the charges that were made against him, but the Society were not convinced, and in 1745 he was dismissed from their service as "unfit to be employed" by them. He apparently continued to live in Pennsylvania after his dismissal, but his eventual fate is unknown.

Chapter IX
NEW ENGLAND

The 18th century saw an increasing proportion of the clergy coming from amongst the colonists themselves. Nevertheless, a significant number of Scots were still continuing to cross the Atlantic to minister to the thirteen colonies. In Virginia in 1776, for example, of the seventy one clergy resident there whose place of birth was known, just over half had been born in the colony, whilst one-fifth of them were natives of Scotland, a figure which did not take into account, of course, men of Scottish descent, born in the colonies.

The three geographical areas – New England, the Middle Colonies and the Southern Colonies – each provided a very different ecclesiastical and political setting. By and large, Anglicans in New England were High Church and Tory. In the Southern Colonies they tended to be Latitudinarian and Whig; whilst in the Middle Colonies there was a mixture of them all. Initially the most difficult area for Anglican clergy to establish themselves in was that of New England, not least because of the Puritan background of the colonists. Yet, paradoxically, it was there that the Church emerged most strongly from the American Revolution.

Some of the migrant Scottish Clergy – men like Blair, Keith, Gordon, and the heroic Mohawk missioners – left a lasting mark upon the developing Church. Most of them though, simply exercised a faithful pastoral ministry, often under conditions of isolation and considerable hardship. They left behind some fascinating glimpses of what it was like to be an Anglican clergyman in eighteenth century colonial America. This is a representative cross section of some of those glimpses.

James Honyman

In 1701 there were only two Anglican clergymen ministering in New England, and those were both at Boston, Massachusetts.

Four years later, the first resident SPG Missionary arrived in Rhode Island. He was The Revd. James Honyman, a Scot, who had spent a short time, immediately before, in the colony of New York. He had first gone to Jamaica, Long Island, to take the place of Patrick Gordon, the young Scottish priest who had accompanied James Keith, and who had died in 1702 within a couple of weeks of his landing in America.

Honyman's arrival at Newport, Rhode Island in 1705 began a New England ministry that was to last for almost half a century. It was not an easy assignment. He was met with opposition from the residents, and with "frowns and discouragements" from the Government, there being "only one baptised Christian in the whole legislature of the Island".

He found a handful of Church people amongst a hostile majority of "Quakers, Anabaptists, Independents, Gortonians and Infidels". But his congregation grew; he opened up work in six other centres, two of which became separate parishes. In

Providence, Rhode Island, the congregation was so numerous that no building could hold them, and he had to preach in the open fields. He helped the congregation there to raise money for building a church, and he himself built a much larger one at Newport at a cost of £2,000.

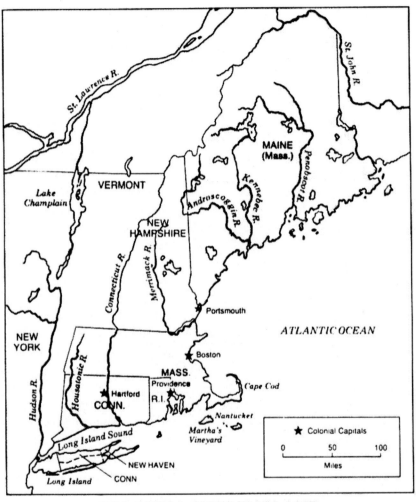

COLONIAL NEW ENGLAND

Altogether, Honyman exercised a solid faithful ministry, not only building up the church in Rhode Island, but also gathering several congregations in Connecticut and Massachusetts. He continued to minister to them until they were able to be provided with their own resident clergy. In 1732 he was writing back to the Society:-

"Between New York and Boston, a distance of three hundred miles and wherein are many Missions, there is not a congregation of the Church of England that can pretend to compare with mine, or equal to it in any respect; nor does any Church consist of members that were of it when I came here, for I buried them all: nor is there any person now alive that did belong to it then, so that our present appearing is entirely owing to the blessing of God and my endeavours to serve Him."

Those endeavours proved extraordinarily fruitful, and included a ministry to native Americans as well as slaves. In 1746 he wrote, in a covering letter for his Notitia Parochialis, that beside "baptising some Indians, I number amongst the congregation above one hundred Negroes who constantly attend the Public Worship."

Honyman died in office in July 1750, having served the Church in the American Colonies for forty-seven years.

George Muirson

In 1705 Honyman was joined in his New England missionary ventures by The Revd. George Muirson who like him, was also a Scot. Muirson had been ordained deacon and priest by the Bishop of London in that year, and immediately after ordination was sent out to Rye in New York Colony. For the rest of his short life he remained at Rye under the auspices of the SPG, although his principal work lay in Connecticut. That work had arisen quite spontaneously.

A few Anglicans at Stratford had written to the rector of Trinity Church in New York asking him to come and conduct services for them from time to time. He was unable to help because of the distance between New York and Stratford, and he passed on the request to Muirson at Rye, who took up the challenge.

Muirson visited Stratford several times in the course of 1706 and again the following year. He was fortunate in being accompanied on these visits by Colonel Caleb Heathcote, one of the most influential men in the colonies and a dedicated Churchman. Without his presence, it is highly probable that Muirson would have found himself in prison in Connecticut. As it was, he met with great difficulty when he tried to exercise his ministry. The small group of Anglicans welcomed him enthusiastically, but when they applied for the use of the public meeting-house to hold their services they were presented with a formidable legal document.

"One of their magistrates with some other officers came to my lodgings, and in the hearing of Colonel Heathcote and a great many people read a long Paper. The meaning of it was to let me know that theirs was a Charter Government, that I had done an illegal thing in coming among 'em to establish a new way of worship, and to forewarn me from preaching any more. This he did by virtue of one of their Laws".

The effect of the persecution was to stir up sympathy for the Church and for Muirson. Other towns in the Colony invited him to come and visit them, and he became in effect an itinerant priest in Connecticut. The tactics of the Independents were repeated:- "They left no means untryed both foul and fair, to prevent the settling of the Church among them – the people were likewise threatened with imprisonment and a forfeiture of £5 for coming to hear me. It would require more time than you would willingly bestow on these lines, to express how rigidly and severely they treat our People, by taking their Estate when they are not willing to support their Ministers. They spare not openly to speak reproachfully and with great contempt of our Church, they say the sign of the Cross is the sign of the Devil and those who receive it are given to the Devil".

Despite all this, Muirson succeeded in gathering together a respectably-sized congregation; so much so that, by the Spring of 1707, they were in a position to ask the SPG for a missionary of their own. They all agreed that the obvious man for the job was the young Scot from Rye. Unfortunately, Muirson died before the petition reached England.

In the meantime, the congregation continued to meet together in spite of their persecution by the civil authorities. They wrote repeatedly to the SPG for a priest, spelling out the difficulties that attended their meeting for worship. They complained that the Independent authorities had demanded a capital levy (a poll tax) from the Anglicans to pay for a manse for an Independent Minister. On refusal, the Anglican churchwarden and a member of the Vestry had been dragged eight miles through the snow to the common gaol and imprisoned there until the payments had been made. The Anglicans had appealed to the courts in vain. Even the local tradesmen had boycotted them.

It was six years before a priest was sent to Stratford, and then he only stayed for a short period although they received visits from itinerant clergy from time to time. Ultimately, in 1722, fifteen years after Muirson's death, a permanent resident replacement arrived. Muirson's labours had not been in vain. The replacement was able to write to the SPG: "Our cause flourishes mightily in this country, indeed so much so, that our neighbours look on in astonishment." It was a matter for astonishment that the ministry of a young Scottish priest which had lasted for only two years – and that on a part-time basis – should have borne such fruit.

James McSparran

A great infusion of strength into the Church in New England came from the "conversion" of a number of most able Presbyterian and Congregationalist ministers to Episcopacy. Most prominent among these was the President of Yale College, Timothy Cutler, who with six of his colleagues in 1722 announced their grave doubts about the validity of Presbyterian ordination, a phrase used at the time to include that of the Congregationalist Ministry. The announcement sent an ecclesiastical shock wave throughout New England. Cutler and three of his colleagues applied for ordination in the Church of England and travelled to London for that purpose. One of them died from smallpox in England, but Cutler returned to become the rector of Christ Church, Boston, whilst another went to Stratford (the congregation pioneered by George Muirson) and later became President of King's College (Columbia University).

Two Scots followed the same path. James McSparran was born in Ireland in 1693, the son of Presbyterian parents from Kintore in Argyll. He was educated in Scotland and graduated Master of Arts from the University of Glasgow in 1709. After studying for the Presbyterian ministry, he was admitted as a Licentiate of the Church of Scotland. In 1718, he visited America, staying with a relative in Bristol, at that time within the jurisdiction of the Colony of Massachusetts. He was invited to preach in the local Congregational Church and was afterwards offered the pastorship at a salary of £100 per annum . At that point he appears to have aroused the hostility of a leading Congregationalist, Cotton Mather, who not only delayed McSparran's ordination, but also spread reports that his credentials were fraudulent. In later life, McSparran was to say that a false charge against him as a young man had led him into the Anglican priesthood.

He returned to Britain to seek ordination into the Church of England. In August 1720 he was made deacon by the Bishop of London, and a month later ordained priest in Lambeth Palace Chapel by the Archbishop of Canterbury, with a title "to discharge the ministerial office in the Province of New England". The SPG appointed him as Rector of St. Paul's, Narragansett in Rhode Island and also to officiate at Bristol, Freetown, Swansea and Little Compton. He proved to be one of the most able of all the missionaries sent to America by the Society.

Like Honyman, he had a broadly mixed congregation and was able to report on regular classes of seventy native Americans and slaves who were "given instruction before Divine Service". He was instrumental in establishing an Episcopal Church in New London, Connecticut and was credited with being the catalyst for the conversion from Congregationalism to Anglicanism of Samuel Seabury, senior, the father of the future bishop.

McSparran's sound scholarship was recognised by the University of Oxford who made him an honorary Doctor of Divinity in 1737. He was a controversial author, and his defence of Anglican orders in The Sacred Dignity of the Christian Priesthood Vindicated, published in 1752, raised a storm of protest from non-Anglican ministers in New England.

He campaigned hard for a bishop to be appointed for the colonies, and in fact bequeathed his farm for the use and support of a bishop whose diocese would include the Naragansett country. He died in Rhode Island in 1757 at the age of sixty-four after twenty-six years in the Anglican ministry, all of which had been spent at St. Paul's.

William Hooper

Hooper was born and educated in Scotland. He had emigrated to America about 1734 to take up an appointment as a tutor, and rapidly became involved as a lay minister in the Congregational Church in Boston. He was soon recognised as an exceptionally gifted preacher, and when the West Congregational Church was founded in 1737, he was appointed as its first pastor, being ordained into the ministry in May of that year. His ministry proved to be very acceptable to the congregation, but the rigid Calvinism of Boston apparently made him dissatisfied with the Congregational Church. After a pastorate of nine years, Hooper resigned his cure on the 19 November 1746. The same day he was elected as rector of Trinity Episcopal Church, Boston, conditional upon his receiving Anglican orders. There was a great outcry in both Anglican and congregationalist circles. The previous rector of Trinity had died in England a little over two months before, and the charge was regarded as a "plum" amongst all the Anglican churches in America.

The Governor of Massachusetts, William Shirley, wrote to the Secretary of the SPG, setting out the circumstances of Hooper's appointment:

"Upon Trinity Church's becoming vacant Mr. Hooper took occasion to signify to me, what I thought I could discover before from his declared Sentiments in conversation with him some years since (when I had more leisure to converse than I have now), that he was dispos'd to come over to the Church of England; and I thereupon propos'd his succeeding Mr Davenport in his late Cure, which offer was most readily embrac'd by the proprietors of Trinity Church, who, to make their invitation of him to be their Minister more strong have raised that living from £100 to £110 Sterling a year, and a liberal Collection was made in a few hours for defraying his charges in going to England for Ordination."

Roger Price, the first (and only) Commissary of the Bishop of London to be appointed to New England, took umbrage at what he regarded as the high-handedness of the Governor, coupled with suspicions (shared with some of the Anglican clergy) of Hooper's motives. Commissary Price wrote to the Bishop of London (four days after the Governor had written):

"I thought it my duty to inform your Lordship that Mr Hooper late a dissenting teacher, is going to England with a design of receiving Episcopal Ordination, being appointed by the Congregation of Trinity Church to succeed Mr Davenport. His change has been so unusual and sudden as to allow me no time to know his true character, which has come to me hitherto only by common report. This indeed has not been at all favorable to him, either in respect of his principles or morals. I told him this when he came to me for a recommendation to your Lordship, and for this reason refused it, whereupon after some threatening language, he left me. The Governor and several Gentlemen espouse his cause very warmly, but I have not spared to tell them it was my opinion that instead of increasing the number of

Churchmen, by taking such suspicious ministers into the Church, it might rather be a means of destroying Christianity which is already in this town too much tinctured with base opinions. My Brethren of the Clergy whom I have advised upon this affair have unanimously concurr'd in these sentiments. I have committed this letter to the care of The Revd. Mr Woods, Chaplain to the Chester Man of War, a Gentleman who has Preached for some time in Trinity Church, and behaved himself to the General approbation; he can further inform your Lordship what was said in the conversation of the Clergy upon this subject."

Price's judgement proved to be wrong. The Bishop of London was satisfied as to Hooper's character and motives; he was ordained in 1747 and inducted as Rector of Trinity Church, Boston, in August of that year. He spent almost twenty years at Trinity and his rectorship was apparently just as fruitful as his nine years in the West Congregational Church had been.

William Smith

An interesting Scottish priest, who had a somewhat chequered ministry, was William Smith. (Not to be confused with the other William Smith, who became Provost of the University of Pennsylvania). They were both Aberdonians, and had both received their university education in that city. This Smith was born in 1762 and was ordained in the Scottish Episcopal Church before moving to America in 1785. Two years later, he became rector of St. Paul's, Narragansett, where Dr. James McSparran had been one of his predecessors.

After three years at St. Paul's, he moved to Trinity Church, Newport, where he spent nine years, taking an active part in the organisation of the diocese of Rhode Island. Yet another move followed to St. Paul's, Connecticut in 1787, the year in which he preached at the consecration of The Revd. Abraham Jarvis as second Bishop of Connecticut, in succession to Samuel Seabury. He resigned his living in 1800, and spent the next twenty-one years until his death in a variety of teaching and supply posts. A contemporary described him as "a man of extensive and diversified learning, of an ardent and fertile mind, a great and ready command of languages, a flow of thought, as well extemporaneously and in conversation as on paper. He had moreover deep religious feelings, unquestionable zeal and devotion to his duties, whether in religious or secular instruction, and a frank, kind disposition. Yet, unhappily, he was never successful in either sphere of labour, in any proportion to his ability or acquirements."

Smith was an accomplished musician and published several books intended for the use of organists and church choirs, which had a widespread influence on the development of Church music, particularly within the Episcopal Church. In another age, he might have been the provincial chairman of the Royal School of Church Music. One lasting claim to remembrance was his contribution of the "Office of

Institution of Ministers" to the Episcopalian Book of Common Prayer, composed originally at the request of the Connecticut clergy, and later adopted with only slight modification by the General Convention of the Protestant Episcopal Church of the United States of America.

George Bissett

One Scottish priest who had served in New England was destined to play a small but important role in the approach to the Scottish bishops concerning the consecration of Dr. Samuel Seabury. He was The Revd. George Bissett whose part in that approach is described in Chapter X.

Bissett was born and brought up in Peterhead, Aberdeenshire, where he was a parishioner of Robert Kilgour, who later became Primus of the Scottish Church and who was the chief consecrator at Seabury's episcopal ordination in 1784. Bissett had been a student at Marischal College, Aberdeen, graduating Master of Arts in 1759. One of his contemporaries at Marischal was Arthur Petrie, a co-consecrator with Kilgour.

After graduation, Bissett taught for a time in Kensington, London, before emigrating to America, where he was appointed incumbent of Trinity, Newport, Rhode Island, the church whose first priest had been James Honyman. When the War of Independence broke out Bissett became a Loyalist refugee. He returned to Britain taking up residence in London, where he renewed his association with James Elphinstone in whose school he had taught a quarter of a century earlier. Bissett and Elphinstone co-operated in the approach to Scotland; Bissett's earlier relationships with Kilgour and Petrie no doubt helping to smooth the path.

Bissett's final pastoral appointment was at St. John's, New Brunswick in Canada, where he went as an SPG missionary in 1786. He had a short ministry there, dying two years later, greatly mourned by the congregation of St. John's. They wrote to the Society in London; "No Church or Congregation ever suffered a severer misfortune in the death of an incumbent than we (of St. John's) experienced in the loss of this eminent Servant of Christ, the best and most amiable of men, Mr Bissett."

William McGilchrist

The Revd. William McGilchrist was born in Scotland in 1703. He graduated from Balliol College, Oxford in 1731 and was ordained deacon in 1733, priest in 1735. After serving in St. Philip's church, Charleston, South Carolina for four years from 1741, he returned to London. The following year he was appointed rector of St. Peter's, Salem, Massachusetts.

The Wardens of St. Peter's, in writing to the SPG in February 1745 had this to report: "As this town is the Shire town of the County and the next Market Town to

Boston in New England, you can conclude our Opposition has been great." "The Society replied the following year, after McGilchrist's appointment: "The Society expect and insist that you keep up your promised Salary of 130 pounds p. annum, and more over provide him with some land for a Glebe, it being lately settled as a Standing Rule by the Society, that they will appoint no Missionaries to any Church, before there is a House and Glebe provided for him."

McGilchrist settled in happily at Salem, and his ministry proved to be a fruitful one. The congregation increased to such an extent that it became necessary to extend the length of the church building by twenty feet. After two years he could report that one hundred and ten heads of families were members of St. Peter's.

However, the storm clouds of The Revolution were gathering. In the same year, he wrote to the Society in London: "The minds of people in this country are much enflamed at present on account of the Parliament taxes on glass, paper etc. to raise a Revenue." Over the next couple of years, the political situation began to look bleaker for Episcopalians. St. Peter's, as elsewhere, became a target for the angry populace.

McGilchrist continued to exercise his public duties until February 1777, when he was forced to close the church building and the parish ceased to function. Stones had been thrown through the windows of the church during the times of divine service and many of the church members received rough treatment at the hands of the mob.

The rector's health failed rapidly, undoubtedly aggravated by the darkening political situation, and he died in 1770 at the age of sixty-seven. His ministry in Salem had covered a period of twenty-four years.

Chapter X
ESTABLISHMENT AND THE STRUGGLE FOR THE EPISCOPATE

REPELLING THE EPISCOPATE
From a Contemporary Print

In December 1824, The Revd. Walter Farquhar Hook (then a curate of Whippingham in the Isle of Wight, but later to become vicar of Leeds, and the most notable parish priest in the Church of England) wrote to his father, the Archdeacon of Huntingdon: "Is Government friendly to the Episcopalians of Scotland? When has it proved itself so? Has it not always been the policy of every Government, Whig or Tory, to oppress, persecute, exterminate the Episcopal Church? Was not even their bare toleration merely wrung from it, with a Lord Chancellor haranguing vehemently against them? But even look further, when the greatest and wisest and best of our prelates, when Wake and Potter and Secker, names ever to be honoured, were earnest with Government to permit bishops without temporal rank to be sent to our colonies, what did the Government do? It treated the application with contempt; or was deterred by political circumstances. It has been the work of nearly a century to wring from the government permission to send bishops to our colonies."[1]

In fact, Hook was understating the case. It had been the work of nearly two centuries to obtain consent for the foundation of colonial bishoprics. The question of resident bishops in America had been raised as early as 1638, when Archbishop William Laud had endeavoured to send a bishop to Virginia.[2] It was to become one of the major issues in ecclesiastical politics during the eighteenth century, and the struggle for bishops to minister to Anglicans in other parts of the world spilled over well into the nineteenth century. No realistic assessment of Scotland's contribution to the development of the Anglican Communion can fail to take into account that struggle for the episcopate outside the British Isles. The miracle is that Anglicanism survived at all as anything other than the Church of England by law established.

THE HISTORICAL BACKGROUND

Opposition to the appointment of bishops for the colonies came from both the government at home and from within the colonies themselves. The restoration of the Church of England as the established Church had brought with it a retention of much of "the pernicious mediaeval heritage. The bishop was still an officer of state, a member of the House of Lords; he still had certain powers of coercive jurisdiction. He was not so much a Father in God as a judge, entrusted primarily with the task of maintaining discipline and repressing disorder."

From 1714 until 1760, the Whigs were in power. They were warmly supported by the English bishops, most of whom as the years went by, owed their preferment to the party in power. A few still continued to hold diplomatic or political office. All of them were closely bound up with Parliament, forming a considerable proportion of

the House of Lords, looking upon their membership of the Upper House as a matter of obligation. This meant residence in London for more than half the year, with the consequent financial burden of maintaining a town house as well as a palace in their cathedral city. The endowments of the sees were large, and on top of that, many of the bishops were pluralists, holding deaneries or prebends in commendam to supplement their incomes, whilst paying a small stipend to a curate to exercise the cure of souls.

The method of appointing bishops did not inspire much confidence. A royal congé d'élire to a Dean and Chapter requiring the election of a crown nominee on the recommendation of government ministers did not accord well with the kind of democratic methods towards which some of the colonies were working.3

The Establishment connection, the political involvement and the trappings of palaces and wealth had obscured the true nature of episcopacy. In fact, none of those things had anything to do with being a bishop per se, and they were as far removed as can be imagined from the modest houses, the pitifully low stipends, and the total absence of outward display of the Scottish bishops. Nevertheless, it was the image of the English episcopate that was uppermost in people's minds, and the memory of it that the colonists (and particularly the dissenters) carried with them and perpetuated.

Another memory that they took with them when they left England was of their treatment after the restoration of Charles II to the throne in 1660. It was almost the mirror-image of the treatment of the Scottish Episcopalians after the Revolution in 1688. Both, in a sense, were following the common pattern of revolution and counter-revolutionary times. The so-called Clarendon Code was a series of Acts of Parliament which penalised those who could not accept the pattern of worship prescribed by the Book of Common Prayer together with the ministry of bishops, priests and deacons. Under the Act of Uniformity of 1662, some two thousand ministers who could not or would not give their "unfeigned consent and assent" to the Prayer Book were ousted from their benefices on St. Bartholomew's Day – the 14 August 1662.4

Power was in the hands of the Cavalier Parliament who remembered the wrongs that they themselves had suffered at the hands of the Roundheads – the execution of Charles I, the ejection of the Anglican clergy when the Puritans were in power, and the time when use of the Prayer Book had been made a criminal offence. Now the boot was on the other foot.

Already, in the year before the Act of Uniformity, the Corporation Act had made it necessary for all holders of public office to receive Holy Communion according to the rites of the Church of England. Three years later, the Conventicle Act of 1664 defined a conventicle as a place where more than five persons assembled for worship. The Five-Mile Act of 1665 made it an offence for an ejected minister to live within five miles of his former town or parish where he had previously ministered.

"The Corporation Act had removed Puritan magistrates; the Act of Uniformity had removed Puritan ministers; the Conventicle Act struck at the rank and file of nonconformity. Anyone over sixteen years of age apprehended at a meeting held under pretext of religious worship, but not conducted according to the liturgy of the Church of England, became subject to the penalties of the Act … In the first instance punishment was to be three months imprisonment or a fine of not more than five pounds; for the second offence the penalties were doubled; on the third occasion, after trial by the jury, the accused was to be sentenced to transportation to one of the American Colonies, Virginia and New England excepted."[5]

In other words, nonconformists or dissenters were second-class citizens, excluded from the only English universities of Oxford and Cambridge. Even after the Revolution of 1688, things were only marginally better. Not surprisingly, those who emigrated to the colonies voluntarily, or who were sent there compulsorily under the Conventicle Act, harboured great bitterness. The Church of England by law established represented both opposition and oppression, and at the heart of that Church were the bishops. The American dissenters were not likely to encourage the settling of bishops in the colonies; as will be seen.

This was not the kind of episcopacy for which the Anglicans overseas were pleading. For some of the dissenters, bishops were a possible form of church government. For Anglicans, they were something to do with the very nature of the church. The introduction to the Ordinal said:- "It is evident unto all men diligently reading Holy Scripture and Ancient authors that from the Apostles' time there have been these Orders of Ministers in Christ's Church:- bishops, priests and deacons." There were then, as there are now, three Anglican views of bishops in relation to the Church, about whether or not they are of the esse, the bene esse or of the plene esse. That is, whether they are essential to the very being of the Church – the Anglo Catholic view; or whether they are a good form of church government – the low-church view; or whether they are the ideal and fullest form of government for the perfection of the Church – the mediating view. The classic Anglican expression, articulated by Archbishop John Bramhall, is the latter, following Launcelot Andrews for whom "some part of the divine law" is missing from non-episcopal churches, but who would not go on to unchurch them. "Nevertheless, if our form (that is episcopacy) be of divine right, it does not follow from thence that there is no Salvation without it. He is blind who does not see churches consisting without it; he is hard-hearted who denies them salvation." Bramhall explained the importance of bishops by "distinguishing between the true nature of and essence of the Church, which we do readily grant, and the integrity of perfection of the Church, which we cannot grant them without swerving from the judgement of the Catholic Church."[6]

Nevertheless, there were later Caroline divines who were of the esse school. Some of them declared that it was not possible to dispense with episcopacy in the historic succession, and that a Church which had done so was not a true Church and had no valid sacraments. Many of the non-jurors fell uneasily between the esse and plene esse schools. For the most part, whatever their theological standpoint, the Anglican colonists wanted bishops on pragmatic grounds – to confirm, to ordain, to govern. What they did not want were replicas of the English episcopate.

After Archbishop Laud's abortive attempt in 1638 to settle a bishop in America, the next plan came in 1672. The Earl of Clarendon then prevailed upon Charles II to nominate a bishop for Virginia, with a general charge over all the other colonies and with Jamestown as his see city. The Church in America was to be placed under the jurisdiction of the Archbishop of Canterbury and within his Province, so that the responsibility of the Bishop of London for the American colonies would cease. The Privy Council concurred, and a charter was drawn up nominating a Scottish priest, The Revd. Dr. Alexander Murray as the first bishop. Letters patent under the Great Seal for his consecration were prepared by Sir Orlando Bridgeman, who was Keeper from 1667 to 1672, but the scheme was frustrated and Murray was never consecrated. The reasons assigned for the failure are various. It may have been due to Clarendon's fall and the opposition of his successors, who set themselves firmly against anything that he had planned. This so-called Cabal derived its name from the initial letters of the names of the five men who ruled absolutely – Lords Clifford and Arlington who were Papists, the Duke of Buckingham an avowed atheist, Sir W. Ashley, a deist, and Lord Lauderdale, a Presbyterian. Archbishop Secker attributed the failure of the Virginia bishopric scheme to the fact that the tax to support it would have fallen on the customs. Yet another reason was attributed to the death of Charles II.[7]

Alexander Murray himself had been a staunch supporter of the Stuart cause and had been present with King Charles at the battle of Worcester in 1651 when an attempt had been made to regain the throne. He had accompanied the king in exile, and had ultimately settled in Virginia, where he became episcopal minister of Ware parish in Gloucester County, and where he ministered until his death. It was a tragedy that this proposal came to nothing – it left the Church in North America without a bishop for more than another hundred years.

As early as September 1703, two years after his arrival in America, John Talbot had written to the SPG on the need for episcopal oversight in the colonies. After praising the work done by George Keith, Talbot went on:-

"It seems the strangest thing in the World, and 'tis thought History can't parallel it, That any Place has received the Word of God so many years, so many hundred Churches built, so many thousand Proselytes made, and still remain altogether in the Wilderness as sheep without a shepherd. The Poor Church of America is worse on't in this respect than any of her Adversaries."

"The Presbiterians here come a great way to lay hands on one Another, but after all I think they had as good stay att home for the good they do!… But the poor Church has nobody upon the Spot to Comfort or Confirm her Children. No body to Ordain several that are willing to serve, were they authorised, for the Work of the Ministry. Therefore they fall back again into the Herd of the Dissenters, rather than they will be att the Hazard and Charge to goe to England for Orders; so that we have seen several Counties, Islands and Provinces which have hardly an Orthodox Minister amongst 'em, which might have been supply'd had we been so happy to see a Bishop or Suffragan apud Americanos."

"We are all satisfied that we can't have a greater Friend and Patron than himself (Bishop Compton). But alas! There is such a great Gulph, fixed between, that we can't pass to him, nor he to us; but may he not send a suffragan?"[8]

Two years later, on 2 November 1705, fourteen clergymen, representing New York, New Jersey and Pennsylvania, assembled at Burlington under Talbot's leadership. Two of the clergy were Swedes in Anglican orders and one was French; of the remaining ten no fewer than six were Scots. They considered gravely the handicaps under which they laboured because of the lack of a bishop in America and decided that they would send a petition to the Archbishops of Canterbury and York, the Bishops' of the Church of England and the Society for the Propagation of the Gospel. Not only that, they considered the matter of such great importance that they determined that Talbot should take passage to England and present in person their petition for a bishop. Part of their communication was as follows:-

"Your Missionaries being convened at Burlington, esteem themselves in duty bound to lay before the Most Reverend, the Right Reverend & Right Honourable Members of the Society, what we conceive to be necessary with God's blessing on our Labours, to promote the ends of our Mission. The presence and assistance of a Suffragan Bishop is most needful to ordain such persons as are fit to be called to serve in the sacred ministry of the Church. We have been deprived of the advantages that might have been received of some Presbyterian and Independent Ministers that formerly were, and of others that are still willing to conform and receive the holy character, for want of a Bishop to give it. The baptised want to be confirmed. The presence is necessary in the councils of these provinces to prevent the inconveniences which the Church labours under by the influences which seditious men's counsels have upon the publick administration and the opposition which they make to the good inclinations of well affected persons; he is wanted not only to govern and direct us but to cover us from the malignant effects of those misrepresentations that have been made by some persons empowered to admonish and inform against us who indeed want admonition themselves."[9]

The appeal found a ready response from the Society for the Propagation of the Gospel. The previous year, after long consideration the SPG had stated a case for the consideration of the Law Officers of the Crown, in which reference was made to the existence of Suffragan Bishops in primitive times, and to their revival by Statute (26 Henry VIII Cap XIII) in 1534. The Society asked for opinion as to whether under this Act:- "the Bishops Suffragan of Colchester, Dover, Nottingham and Hull might be disposed of for the service of the Church in foreign parts and if not, whether the Archbishops and Bishops of the Realm would be liable for any inconvenience or penalties from the Statute or Ecclesiastical laws should they consecrate Bishops for foreign parts with no other jurisdiction but that of Commissary or the like. If so, whether by the Act of Edward VI Cap 2, for the election of Bishops, the Queen might not appoint new Suffragans for foreign parts within her dominions."

The case was entrusted to the Archbishop of Canterbury, Thomas Tenison, President of the SPG. The case was strengthened by the petition from the fourteen clergymen which had been presented by Talbot. In 1707, Tenison laid the matter before Queen Anne, who asked him to submit a plan. The case was supported wholeheartedly by Henry Compton, the Bishop of London. In December of 1705, specifically in response to the Burlington petition, Compton drew up his own Observations. He maintained that there could be no dispute regarding the need for resident bishops in America, "in the present disorders now arising in some of the Plantations as likely to increase to an entire discouragement of the Clergy already there established." The question was, what kind of bishop would be most appropriate? He was realistic about the force of opposition to the proposal in the colonies, knowing "an absolute bishop" would be most improper, would cause great alarm and would lead to innumerable protests to England. The kind of bishop he envisaged was one "who had all the necessary power to restrain vice and keep good order, but no more". He would be in much the same position as a Commissary (and the colonies were accustomed to that office) but he would have the added power to consecrate churches, to ordain and to confirm. "It will be the safest way at first for a proof how it will take among them, and all the faults and defects may more easily be corrected and amended; because it will not be near so troublesome to question and remove a Suffragan Bishop as another; nor will his being put out of office be near so inconvenient. Besides, the beginning of any new establishment ought to be carried out gradually, which will make all steps easier and in case of Disappointment, the matter will not be so grievous."10

Despite Tenison's presentation and the support of Compton and the SPG, the whole matter of a bishop for the colonies hung fire. In 1709, Compton again represented to the Society "the very great inconveniences attending its affairs – for want of a Bishop to govern the Church in the Plantations". The following year, the Society itself represented to the Queen "the earnest and repeated desires, not only of the missionaries, but of divers other considerable persons that are in communion with our excellent Church to have a Bishop settled in your plantations as being very useful and necessary for establishing the Gospel in those parts."

In 1712, on the motion of Lord Clarendon, the Society prepared "the draught of a Bill proposed to be offered in Parliament for the establishment of Bishops and Bishoprics in America." Parliamentary wheels ground slowly and the death of Queen Anne in 1714 once again frustrated the proposal.

In the meantime John Talbot had again written in 1713 in desperation to the Society:-

"The Rights of the Church are invaded and Possest by her Enemies, affidavits are procured and dispersed by the worst of men against the best Missionaries, the plate and Books given by the Society and other Benefactors are violently carried away, and those who pretend to be Promoters of the Gospel use all wayes and means amongs, and have perswaded one unworthy Brother to carry affidavits from Province to Province agt another, And as I have allways Said wee cannot Expect any better Treatment till we have a Superior Pastor to Order and establish the Church. This is the one thing necessary, which I have been solliciting these ten years. I find it all in vain for them or us to offer to propagate the Gospel or Erect the Church without Bishop or Deacon, which I humbly offer to our Superiors at home, for the burden is too hard upon us poor Presbiters, who labour under all Sorts of Perils and Difficulties which we are not able to bear any longer."[11]

On the accession of George I, the Society made yet another representation to the Crown, in order "to forward the great work of Converting infidels to the saving faith of our Blessed Redeemer, and for the regulating such Christians in their faith and practice as are already converted thereunto," it was highly expedient to establish four bishoprics – two for the islands and one each for Burlington and Williamsburg. However, the 1715 Rising in Scotland, the suspicion (not without foundation) that some of the colonial clergy were Jacobites, and other political problems led once more to the proposal being shelved.

Talbot returned to the fray again in 1716. "I cannot think that the honourable Society had done more if they had found one honest man to bring Gospel orders over to us. No doubt, as they have freely received, they would freely give, but there's a nolo episcopari only for poor America."[12]

Edmund Gibson, who succeeded John Robinson as Bishop of London in 1723, held the See for twenty-five years. He took his responsibilities for the colonies extremely seriously. He obtained a special Commission under Letters Patent from the Crown to exercise a jurisdiction in the colonies, not only that enjoyed by his predecessors under the Order in Council of 1633, but also of coercive jurisdiction over the clergy. He was authorised to appoint commissaries with far wider-ranging powers than those exercised by men like Talbot and Bray. Gibson's commissaries could convene courts, summon clergy to appear before them and give evidence on oath, impose penalties of monition, suspension or even deprivation from office. The procedure in thse courts was on the same lines as those of ecclesiastical courts in England. Gibson also introduced, through his commissaries, a comprehensive system of questionnaires for the colonial clergy.

In 1728 "after investigating the origins and legal bases of his authority as bishop of the Plantations, he drew up his project for the settlement of bishops there. It was somewhat more modest in scope than that presented to Queen Anne in 1713, since he would be content with one bishop for the islands, and if necessary, with one for the mainland." As far as finance was concerned, Gibson thought the bishop might double the job of being in charge of the clergy with that of the principalship of a college. Clergy might help by giving a tithe of their incomes, and help might be secured with grants from the Crown customs. In furtherance of this scheme, he invited the clergy in Maryland to nominate one of their number as bishop, whom he would propose to consecrate as a suffragan to the See of London. The Revd. Dr. John Colebatch was chosen by the clergy, duly nominated to Gibson, and prepared to travel to England. It is not clear whether or not the Bishop had obtained the consent of the Crown or of the Privy Council to his plans. However, before Colebatch could leave, the Maryland Courts prevented his departure by issuing a writ of ne exeat regno. That effectively put an end to the plans. The Commission which Gibson had obtained lapsed on his death in 1748. His successors took no steps to renew it, and so the jurisdiction of the Bishops of London over the colonies reverted to what it had been prior to 1723.[13]

It was not that they were disinterested. Thomas Sherlock, Gibson's successor, felt so strongly that the colonies should have their own bishop that he was most reluctant to exercise authority over them, which is why he never asked for a definite commission as Gibson had done. He made vigorous efforts to secure a bishop; he approached the king and his ministers, he sent an emissary to sound out opinion in America, he made a direct appeal to the Duke of Newcastle. In this he was ably assisted by Joseph Butler (Bishop of Bristol from 1738 to 1750, of Durham 1750 to 1752). In 1750, Butler drew up parameters of the powers that colonial bishops should exercise, in the hope that this would remove apprehensions that such bishops would pose a threat to other religious communities in America:-

"i/ That no coercive power is desired over the laity in any case, but only a power to regulate the behaviour of the clergy who are in Episcopal Orders, and to correct and punish them according to the laws of the Church of England, in case of misbehaviour or neglect of duty, with such power as the commissaries abroad have exercised.

That nothing is desired for such bishops that may in the least interfere with the dignity or authority, or interest of the Governor, or any other Officer of State. Probate of wills, licences for marriages, etc. to be left in the hands where they are; and no share in the temporal government is desired for bishops.

The maintenance of such bishops not be at the charge of the colonies.

No bishops are intended to be settled in places where the Government is left in the hands of Dissenters, as in New England etc. but authority to be given only to ordain clergy for such Church of England congregations as are among them, and to inspect into the manners and behaviour of the said clergy and to confirm the members thereof".[14]

All these overtures were rejected. The cause was taken up by Thomas Secker (Bishop of Oxford 1737 – 1758 and Archbishop of Canterbury 1759 – 1768). Secker had long had an interest in the colonial episcopate. In a sermon before the SPG in 1740 he had reviewed the work done by the Society and the hindrances which it had found to its progress. "And had they bishops there, those persons might be ordained without the inconveniences of a long Voyage. Vacancies might be supplied in much less time; the primitive and useful Appointment of Confirmation might be restored; and an orderly Discipline exercised in the Churches. Nor would such an Establishment encroach at all on either a Liberty of Conscience, which ought ever to be sacredly preserved; or on the present Civil Rights, either of the Governors or of the Peoples in our Colonies".15

In 1766, a fresh voice was added to the pleading. It came from The Revd. Charles Inglis, the priest of Scottish descent newly appointed to Trinity Church, New York. It followed the tragic death of two newly-ordained young clergymen who were to have succeeded Inglis in Dover and Mispillion, and who had travelled to London for ordination and had been drowned on the return passage. The following extract is from a letter sent to the Secretary of the SPG:-

"This Moment I received Information of a Vessel which is to sail from this port tomorrow for London; & am extremely sorry for the disagreeable News I have to acquaint you of, by the Opportunity – viz, the Loss of The Revd. Messrs. Giles & Wilson, appointed by the Society to succeed me in the Mission of Dover & Mispillion, who were shipwrecked & drowned on the Coast of America on Sunday the 6th Inst.

"I am greatly distressed about the Mission of Dover. There is the most pressing Necessity that it should be immediately supplied. I do not know of any Person here that intends to take Orders soon; & therefore I earnestly request, You, Dear Sir, to use your Interest with the Society to have the Missions filled as soon as possible – that Dover at least may be supplied.

"The Expence and Hazard in going to England for Orders were always discouraging Circumstances. This melancholy Accident will increase our Apprehension of Danger, & shews they are well founded. Nothing but our having Bishops here can remove these and many other Grievances which the American Churches labour under.

"Our having Bishops here on the Terms we want them, is a Thing so equitable in itself, & so essential to the Interest of Religion & our Church, that I am lost in Astonishment at our being deprived of them so long. Why are we denied the common Privileges of all other Subjects? Or why are we distinguished by Grievances & Persecutions to which all other Denominations are perfect Strangers?"16

Five years later an appeal came from the Connecticut clergy. "Viewing", they began, "the distressed and truly pitiable state of the Church of England in America, being destitute of resident bishops, we beg leave to renew our addresses in behalf of it … we apprehend it a matter of great importance considered in every view, that the Church should be supported in America … But this Church cannot be supported long in such a country as this, where it has so many and potent enemies, thirsting after universal dominion, and so many difficulties to surmount, without an episcopate, which in any country is essential to the well-being of the Church. Must it not then be surprising and really unaccountable that the Church should be denied the episcopate she asks, which is so necessary to her well-being, and so harmless, that her bitterest enemies acknowledge it can injure none? While Roman Catholics in one of his Majesty's colonies are allowed a bishop, and the Moravians are indulged the same favour in another; nay, and every blazing enthusiast throughout the British Empire is tolerated in the full enjoyment of every peculiarity of his sect, what have the sons of the Church in America done, that they are treated with such neglect, and are overlooked by government? Must not such a disregard of the Church here be a great discouragement to her sons? Will it not prevent the growth of the Church, and thereby operate to the disadvantage of religion and loyalty. We believe episcopacy to be of divine origin, and judge an American episcopate to be essential to the well-being of religion here".17

The Connecticut clergy not only addressed their appeal to the Bishop of London. They sent two of their number – The Revd. Robert McKean and The Revd. Dr. Myles Cooper (President of King's College, New York and afterwards Minister of an Episcopal Chapel in Edinburgh, Scotland) – to sound out the views of other states. This was the first concerted effort made to obtain the views of the whole Anglican Church in America. But the time was too late. The tide of Independence was rising in the wake of the Stamp Act of 1763, and the time was certainly not propitious for anything that savoured of tightening the links with those responsible for this imposition.

The Anniversary Sermon of the SPG preached in 1771 by Robert Lowth (Bishop of Oxford 1766 – 1777 and of London from 1778 to 1787) was, in effect, a post-mortem on the treatment of the American Church. He represented the colonists as being deprived of "the common benefit, which all Christian Churches, in all ages, and in every part of the world, have freely enjoyed; and which in those Countries Christians of every other denomination do at this time freely enjoy... The proper and only remedy hath long since been pointed out: the appointment of one or more resident Bishops, for the exercise of office purely Episcopal in the American Church of England; for administering the solemn and edifying rite of Confirmation; for ordaining Ministers; and superintending their conduct; offices to which the members of the Church of England had an undeniable claim, and from which they cannot be precluded without manifest injustice and oppression". But the undeniable claims had been denied. It was finally the country's independence which was to bring "the common benefit which all Christian Churches have freely enjoyed."18

Chapter XI
SOME CONSEQUENCES OF NO BISHOP
JOHN TALBOT

The increasingly desperate tone of the pleas coming from American clergy can be gauged from the letters quoted, which represent a random selection of the approaches made to the Church of England during the course of the eighteenth century. Before examining the English response, however, two consequences of the policy should be noted; one potentially damaging and the other of lasting effect on the Anglican cause. Since the mother church seemed either powerless or unwilling to act herself, it is not altogether surprising that there was a temptation to act independently of the Church of England in the matter of the episcopate.

One priest who succumbed to the temptation was John Talbot. After the return to England of George Keith in 1704, Talbot had become the senior missionary of the Society for the Propagation of the Gospel. He was very much the doyen of Episcopal clergy, and was known then and afterwards as "the Apostle of New Jersey". His concern to obtain a bishopric for America had led him to approach the SPG as early as 1703. Thereafter he maintained a constant litany of petitions on the subject to the headquarters of the Society. Not only that, he had even journeyed to England in 1706-7 to present in person to the Bishop of London and to the Society the representations of the Burlington clergy. It was an expensive and hazardous undertaking – the passage money alone was more than the equivalent of a year's stipend. Notwithstanding the failure of the mission, Talbot continued to press for the appointment of a bishop during almost the whole of the next twenty years.

In or about the year 1722, The Revd. Robert Welton, D.D. was deprived of the rectorship of Whitechapel, London, because of his adherence to the non-jurors. At that time the non-jurors were in great disfavour because of their allegiance to the Stuart cause. A year later, he had been consecrated by Ralph Taylor, a non-juring bishop. The act of consecration by Taylor alone, acting on his own authority, was irregular, and Welton was never recognised as a bishop in the Church of God by any of the other non-jurors. He therefore travelled to Philadelphia, and functioned as a locum priest for nearly two years, before an order was received recalling him to England. The writ was duly served and Welton left Philadelphia though not for England but Portugal, where he was last heard of in Lisbon.

Before travelling to Philadelphia from London, Welton had joined with Dr. Taylor in raising John Talbot to the episcopate. Talbot had come to London to make certain arrangements with the SPG about his retirement and the possibility of a pension out of the interest from a sum of money left by Archbishop Thomas Tenison for endowing an American bishopric. There seems to be no doubt that the consecration did take place. Potentially it could have been disastrous for the colonial Church.

However, there is no record of any ordinations either by Talbot or by Welton, although there probably were some confirmations. It is certain that neither of the two men acted as episcopi vagantes, and on Talbot's death in 1727 at the age of eighty-two, the American non-juring line was dead. It says much for his restraint that no real damage was done, and the verdict of his biographer, Edgar Legare Pennington, puts the matter in prospective:- "Talbot seems to rise superior to the charges of his critics. His long years of untiring service and self-sacrifice, his patient pursuit of an ideal, his indefatigable efforts to extend the Church and to make it a vital influence throughout the eastern colonies, his irreproachable integrity and morality, have established a name which will not be marred perceptibly by a single mistake committed at the age of nearly eighty. For it may be admitted that the acceptance of Non-Juror consecration was a mistake, an indiscretion: yet there is not the slightest reason to suspect that the old man had any selfish or disloyal intention in mind. He believed that the very existence of the Church in America depended on the presence of a resident bishop: he knew at first hand – far better than the Anglican hierarchy or the Society knew – that the Church was suffering because of its handicaps; that ministers were scarce and hard to obtain, that disorganization was a present menace, and that the dissenting bodies were rapidly overtaking the Church. The need of such a bishop was a constant theme of his correspondence; at his instance, conventions drafted resolutions appealing for a colonial episcopate; he spared himself no pains in the matter of a bishop's dwelling. The long delays, and the lack of any response on the part of the government and the Society must have given him untold anxiety and disappointment. Is it not probable that he turned to the Non-Jurors in desperate hope that he might be permitted to do even a little bit in America to aid the cause?"1

THE METHODISTS

Of much more lasting significance was the action of John Wesley in 1784. Like John Talbot, Wesley was approaching the end of his life when he laid hands on Dr. Thomas Coke and "set him apart" as a superintendent for the Methodist Connexion in America. As Charles Wesley's biographer suggests, "enfeebled by the weight of fourscore years and two, he was persuaded by some of those into whose Hands he was about to drop the reins which in his vigour none had ever shared with him, to attempt to give that which he had never received – the power of ordination. He found in Dr. Coke one who, with much zeal and piety, was predisposed by strong personal vanity to receive gladly the pretended consecration, and who even pressed strongly on Wesley 'his earnest wish' to obtain it". The step was duly taken in Bristol in September 1784, and Wesley "set apart" Coke, instructing him that Francis Astbury, who had been a Methodist leader in America since 1771, should be a fellow superintendent.2

John Wesley's brother Charles was with him in Bristol at the time, but he was not made privy to these plans. He was distressed at what happened, and his epigram written after "the setting apart" expresses his feelings:

Wesley himself and friends betrays
By his own sense forsook:
While suddenly his hands he lays
On the hot head of Coke.
So easily are bishops made,
By man's or woman's whim;
Wesley his hands on Coke hath laid
But – who laid hands on him?3

Coke went to America, and Mr. Astbury was joined in the superintendency with him, the co-consecrators being Coke and a German minister. The Methodists had gone into open schism and it was not long before the superintendents had become bishops.

John Wesley's rationale was explained by Samuel Wilberforce sixty years later:-

"The reasons given by John Wesley for this step bear no marks of his vigorous understanding. At home, he still declares, he would not suffer it; but where there were 'no bishops with legal jurisdiction' his scruples were at an end. He seemed to himself "to violate no order, and invade no man's right, by appointing and sending labourers into the harvest". Every Churchman sees at once the vanity of such excuses. In admitting the power of bishops he sealed his own condemnation. For if such an order did exist in the Church at all, possessed of powers and functions specially committed to it by the Lord, Wesley could not at his own desire arm himself with its peculiar gifts. Yet, whilst we see the weakness of his reasoning, it is most instructive to mark on what he grounded the lawfulness of his usurpation. Here, as elsewhere, it is to the want of bishops that the injury may be distinctly traced."4

Coke's "setting apart" was on 2 September 1784. On the 14 November that year, Samuel Seabury was consecrated in Aberdeen. The following April, Charles Wesley wrote to The Revd. Dr. Thomas Chandler of New Jersey (an early advocate of the American episcopate):-

"What will become of those poor sheep in the wilderness, the American Methodists? How have they been betrayed into a separation from the Church of England, which their preachers and they no more intended than the Methodists here? Had they had patience a little longer, they would have seen a real primitive bishop in America, duly consecrated by three Scotch bishops, who had their consecration from the English bishops, and are acknowledged by them the same as ourselves. There is, therefore, not the least difference betwixt the members of Bishop Seabury's Church and the members of the Church of England."

"You know I had the happiness to converse with that truly apostolical man, who is esteemed by all that knew him, as much as by you and me. He told me he looked upon the Methodists as sound members of the Church, and was ready to ordain any of the preachers whom he shall find duly qualified. His ordination would be genuine, valid and episcopal. But what are your poor Methodists now? Only a new sect of Presbyterians. And after my brother's death, which is now so very near, what will be their end? They will lose all their usefulness and importance."₅

Charles Wesley's prognostication was wrong, but the split was an immense weakening of Anglican witness, which an earlier American episcopate might well have avoided.

WHY NOT BISHOPS?

There were three main pressures against the appointment of bishops for the colonies. The first, and most easily disposed of, was the matter of finance. Who would pay for the American episcopate? The second – a political – pressure came from the colonists themselves, mainly from organised Dissent which was, in turn passed on to England. The third, and most intransigent, opposition came from the British Government, as Walter Hook's comment at the beginning of his chapter so clearly indicated.

FINANCE

The question of finance was raised on both sides of the Atlantic. In the colonies, there may well have been a real anxiety as to whether or not Anglican bishops would become a charge on the taxes and customs paid by non-Anglicans. There was much less justification for opposition on this score in England. Both the SPG and successive bishops of London had assured the Government that the creation of an American bishopric would not entail a charge on the colonies. The New England clergy, too, had proposed in 1750 "The maintenance of such bishops not to be a charge of the colonists", an assurance that was communicated to the Government by Joseph Butler, the Bishop of Durham.6

Henry Compton, when Bishop of London, had proposed that a bishopric be combined with the principalship of a college in order to meet the stipend. The SPG would themselves meet the cost as of an ordinary missionary presbyter. It was unlikely, in any event, that a colonial bishop's stipend would greatly exceed that of other clergy, much after the pattern of the Scottish bishops, with whose circumstances many of the colonial clergy would be familiar. In addition to all that, money had been forthcoming for the endowment of a bishopric. Thomas Tenison, Archbishop of Canterbury, had bequeathed £1,000 in 1717; an anonymous benefactor had given £1,000 in 1727; and Archbishop Thomas Secker had done the same in 1768. Two further gifts of £500 each had come from Mr. Dugald Campbell and from Lady Elizabeth Hastings. The Revd. Dr. James McSparran, the Scottish priest serving in New England, left his farm for the benefit of a bishop whose diocese included the town of Naragansett within its boundaries. Sir William Johnston, "Sole Superintendent of the Affairs of the Six Nations", made a gift of twenty thousand acres of land some thirty miles from Schenectady, intended for the endowment of an episcopate "Subject to His Majesty's grant".[7]

As for accommodation, the SPG had purchased a Bishop's house as early as 1713. It was located in Burlington, New Jersey, "in the sweetest situation in the world, well-built, but ill-contrived and land enough". John Talbot's letters to the Secretary of the Society drew repeated attention to the disrepair into which the house was falling because no bishop had been appointed to occupy it.

It is apparent from all this that it would have been perfectly possible to support and house a bishop without charge falling on either the colonists themselves or the British Government. But the Government seemed not to hear, and it was almost impossible to convince the dissenting colonists of this. Bishops had become bogeymen with which to alarm the adults and terrify the children. Alexander Griswold, who became Presiding Bishop of the American Episcopal Church, recalled: "One of my neighbours who was born in 1745, told me that when a child, he was taught that if Bishops should come into this country, they would take from the people a tenth of everything, children not excepted; and as he happened to be the tenth child of his parents, it was then, he said, his ardent desire that he might immediately die, in case a Bishop were permitted to set foot on our shores". In New England there was a concerted campaign against "all the pomp, grandeur, luxury and regalia of an American Lamebeth": whilst in Virginia there were straightforward demands to know "how much it would cost and who would pay".[8]

OTHER OPPOSITION FROM THE COLONIES

The real difficulty was that the colonists thought of bishops in a way that was entirely foreign to that of the Anglicans who were pressing so earnestly for them. The churchmen based their claims on a purely spiritual conception, looking for that "free, valid and purely ecclesiastical" episcopate later associated with Samuel Seabury's consecration at the hands of the Scottish Bishops. They were concerned with the esse and plene esse of the church. Their concern was sometimes honestly misunderstood, and sometimes wilfully perverted for political ends, with the ulterior motive of inflaming the minds of people against the British Government in the mother country. The general ground of opposition in the thirteen colonies was that the proposed episcopate would import into America part of the system of English Government from which they had so far been spared, but which they associated historically with memories of religious and political oppression from which their ancestors had suffered in Britain and from which they had only escaped by emigration.

Samuel Seabury's descendant and memorialist, Dr. William Jones Seabury, sums

up well the sometimes spurious, and sometimes genuine, opposition to bishops, which was at least as much political as it was religious:-
"The Bishop was conceived of as a State official, empowered under pretence of spiritual jurisdiction to meddle with their customs of worship, and to sit in judgement upon their religious convictions: as connected with a system of legal administration which touched not only spiritual but also temporal rights; and as possessing so exalted a station as to require costly and luxurious provision for its maintenance, the expense of which was to be met by commensurate and general taxation. It was indeed often and patiently explained to those who entertained this conception that it was wholly inapplicable to such an Episcopate as was desired; but whether not convinced, or convinced against their will, they still persisted in entertaining it.9
"It is easy to understand how such objections would take their place among the other contentions which were at the same time being made against what were claimed to be unjust impositions upon the Colonists on the part of the Mother Country, and that assaults upon the Episcopacy would come to be pressed not so much on religious as on political grounds, and from political scruples. In short, the Colonial Episcopate became conspicuous amongst the grievances, real or imaginary, existing or anticipated, which formed the political capital of the opposition party in the Colonies; and war was waged upon it not only by controversial attacks in this Country, but also by influence brought to bear against it in England, which effectively prevented the Civil Sanction which its friends here vainly sought to procure for it."

OPPOSITION IN BRITAIN

The proposal to set up a colonial bishopric was firmly supported by the Society for the Propagation of the Gospel, by successive Archbishops of Canterbury and by Bishops of London. The real resistance came from the Government, and as William Seabury suggested, the influence of organised Dissent spread from the colonies to Westminster. To some extent, the seeds of opposition fell on fertile parliamentary ground. The Church of England had never previously sent bishops overseas, and to members of the House of Lords as of the Commons, the very idea was not only novel but unthinkable. The Church of England was the principal social institution in the land, and its existence was taken for granted. Bishops were amongst the chief officers of State, and their pronouncements were taken as authoritative. But they were not for export.

Much of the influence on government ministers came from the Protestant Dissenting Deputies, a lay committee founded in 1732. They were representative of the Presbyterians, the Independents and the Baptists in the colonies, and managed to acquire a right of access to the throne. When their Chairman enquired of the Lord Chancellor in 1750 about the "danger" of having bishops in America, he was told that there was no danger of such a scheme ever taking place.10

When Bishop Sherlock communicated his plans for a colonial bishopric to government ministers they were summarily refused. "The rejection of those overtures was due to political causes. The true reason of the Bishop of London being opposed and defeated in his scheme of sending bishops was this. "It was that the Duke of Newcastle, Mr. Pelham and Mr. Onslow, can have the interest and votes of the whole body of dissenters upon condition of their befriending them; and by their influence on those persons, the Ministry was brought to oppose it." Such was the statement of Dr. Chandler to Dr. Johnson (both Johnson and Chandler were former Dissenting ministers who had become distinguished SPG missionaries. Both were honoured with Oxford doctorates in divinity).[11]

In 1754, Bishop Secker (then of Oxford) wrote to Dr. Johnson "We have done all we can here in vain, and must wait for more favourable times … so long as they (the Dissenters) are uneasy and remonstrate, regard will be paid to them and their friends here by our ministers of state."

Political considerations continued to outweigh the representations of the American clergy, and of the SPG and bishops. Archbishop Secker in 1766, had this to say: "It is very probable that a Bishop, or Bishops, would have been quietly received in America before the Stamp Act was passed here; but it is certain that we could get no permission here to send one. Earnest and continual endeavours have been used with our successive ministers and ministries, but without obtaining more than promises to consider and confer about the matter; which promises have never been fulfilled. The King (George the Third) hath expressed himself repeatedly in favour of the scheme; and hath promised that, if objections are imagined to lie against other places, a Protestant Bishop should be sent to Quebec where there is a Popish one, and where there are few dissenters to take offence … Incessant application was made to the new ministry; some slight hopes were given, but no step taken."[12]

In the end, it needed a revolution to bring about a change. The revolution came, but it was in Scotland and not in England that the first American bishop was consecrated. The last phrase of this comment from the Protestant Dissenting Deputies after Seabury's return to Connecticut is illuminating: "Since the separation of the two countries, the introduction of Bishops has been partially carried into effect, but with an entire restriction of authority to concerns purely ecclesiastical. The liberal and amicable reception may be considered as a proof that the resistance made by the Dissenters originated in no principles of intolerance towards episcopacy, but simply in a just fear of its influence when allied with temporal power."

Chapter XII
INDEPENDENCE AND ITS CONSEQUENCES

The War of Independence has already been mentioned in connection with Charles Inglis, Samuel Auchmuty and with the ministry of The Revd. John Stuart and his Mohawks. The war followed the revolt of the American colonies against British rule, particularly over the issue of taxation. Hostilities had begun in 1775 when the British and American forces clashed at Lexington and Concord. In 1777, Articles of Confederation agreed in the Continental Congress provided for a Confederation of the thirteen colonies to be known as the United States of America. The war effectively ended with the surrender of the British at Yorktown in 1781, and peace was finally signed at Paris in September 1783.

The Revolution dealt a severe blow to what had been the Church of England in the colonies. However, the eventual outcome of the war was to see the liberation of that Church, and through its link with the Episcopal Church in Scotland to see, too, the real beginning of the Anglican Communion. But at the time, the outlook for the clergy and the congregations must have seemed bleak in the extreme. They were singularly ill-prepared for the situation, not least because there was no episcopate and therefore no spiritual jurisdiction, either to ordain, confirm or act as a focus of unity and discipline. There were those who had been involved in the expulsion of English power, who were determined that the Church of England should go, too. Particularly in Virginia and in Maryland there were occurrences similar to the rabbling of the curates in the west of Scotland a century earlier. Clergy were driven from their cures, churches shut up or sold, and property (contrary to the law) forfeited and sold. The situation in the north was just as bad where the SPG was compelled in terms of its Charter to withdraw its support of clergy. There, too, churches closed and their congregations dispersed.1 Some of the clergy, as in John Stuart's case, went to Nova Scotia, New Brunswick and the Canadas. Others, like Charles Inglis, returned to England.

Samuel Wilberforce, writing in 1844, described the American Church at the end of the war. "The peace which was proclaimed in 1783, found the Church wasted and almost destroyed. The ministrations of the northern clergy had been suspended by their conscientious loyalty; and with the recognition of American Independence the connexion of the missionaries of the venerable society with the land in which they had laboured hitherto was abruptly ended. In the south, its condition was not greatly better. Virginia had entered on the war with one hundred and sixty-four churches and chapels and ninety-six clergymen spread through her sixty-one counties. At the close of the contest, a large number of her churches were destroyed; ninety-four parishes were extinct or forsaken; of the remaining seventy-two, thirty-four were without ministerial services; while of her ninety-one clergymen, only twenty-eight remained. At the time the prospect was indeed depressing. The flocks were scattered and divided; the pastors few, poor and suspected; their enemies dominant and fierce."2 The description might almost have been that of the Scottish Episcopal Church at the same period. The one difference was that the Scottish Church had an episcopate; the American Church had never received one. Independence focused the minds of the clergy and lay people in the United States more than ever before upon the imperative need for bishops if their Church was to survive. It was the culmination of more than a century of pleading.

ALTERNATIVE ROUTES TO AN EPISCOPATE

The prospects were indeed bleak. It was feared that the supply of clergy would cease, as would certainly happen if no bishop were procured for America. No candidates could be ordained by a bishop of the Church of England unless they first took the oath of allegiance to the British crown and no candidate so ordained could be a citizen of the United States without forswearing himself. In fact, two American ordinands were refused ordination on these grounds in 1784, even after making the journey of three thousand miles across the Atlantic.3 As Benjamin Franklin wrote in 1784: "An hundred years hence, when people are more enlightened, it will be wondered at that men in America, qualified by their learning and piety to pray for and instruct their neighbours, should not be permitted to do it until they had made a voyage of six thousand miles out and home to ask leave of a cross old gentleman at Canterbury".

SAMUEL SEABURY
Bishop in Connecticut 1784-1796

If the Church were to continue in the Episcopal tradition with Bishops in the historic succession, there were two possibilities. One was to see if some way could be found to overcome the problem of the oath of allegiance, and so persuade the Church of England bishops to confer episcopal orders on an American citizen. The other possibility was to look elsewhere for the episcopate. The eyes of some American churchmen were turned to the Danish Church. There was, after all, a precedent of Danish clergy ministering under the auspices of the SPCK in South India. In 1784 , Samuel Seabury reported from England that he had heard of some ordination candidates from the Southern States wondering whether to go on to Denmark for their ordination.4 Dr. James Walker, Bishop of Edinburgh, summed up the difficulties about Danish ordinations in a letter written half a century later in 1834:- "The Church in Norway and Denmark is similar in all respects, though deficient in that most important point, the Episcopal succession – which was so little known, that Dr. Seabury, when he failed to obtain consecration in England, was actually in treaty with the Bishop of Zealand. He was better directed to our then almost unknown Church: and this direction was given by Lowth, then Bishop of London, and I have lately heard that the venerable President Routh was the means of directing Bishop Lowth to our Bishops".

("The venerable President" was Dr. Martin Routh, for no less than sixty-three years President of Magdalen College, Oxford, and a staunch friend of the Scottish Episcopal Church. His name appears in the annals of the Scottish Church in connection with the episcopate of Matthew Luscombe).

It seems likely that some kind of quasi-official approach was made to the American Church through the Danish Government. The Archbishop of Canterbury (John Moore) mentioned to Dr. Seabury that some ordinands had met with every encouragement to tempt them to make the voyage to Denmark. That this course was not eventually pursued may well have been the result of a meeting between Samuel Seabury and Dr. Routh. The following account of that meeting is given by Dean J. W. Burgon:-

"Dr. Seabury, whose endeavours with the English Bishops were of necessity unsuccessful, was directed (by Lord Chancellor Thurlow) to repair to Routh at Oxford, with a view to consulting the learned young Divine as to the best source for obtaining valid Consecration, and especially as to the validity of the Danish Succession: Seabury having been himself persuaded in London that he might safely apply to the Bishops of that country. The President of Magdalen was known in after years to refer with excusable satisfaction to his own share in that (and the earlier) memorable interview. "I ventured to tell them, sir, that they would not find there what they wanted." He convinced his auditory on both occasions that the Scandinavian sources – including Norwegian and Swedish as well as Danish – were not trustworthy. It was Routh in short who effectively dissuaded Seabury from the dangerous project: strongly urging upon him at the same time the unimpeachable claims of the Scottish Episcopate, - of whose succession there is no doubt."[5]

One other threat to the "free, valid and purely ecclesiastical episcopacy" which the Americans were seeking, came from Dr. William White, the Chaplain of Congress, and the only Anglican clergyman left in the State of Philadelphia. In an anonymous pamphlet, The Case of the Episcopal Church in the United States Considered written in 1782, he proposed that, for an interim period made necessary by the political situation, episcopacy should be put into a kind of commission analogous to presbyterianism. White was an old-fashioned Low Churchman, and his proposal horrified the High Churchmen further north. It undoubtedly increased the urgency of their search for the historic episcopate. White's pamphlet put the case in this way:-

"It will be said that we ought to continue as we are, with the hope of obtaining episcopacy thereafter. But are the acknowledged ordinances of Christ's holy religion to be suspended for years, perhaps as long as the present generation shall continue, out of delicacy to a disputed point, and that relating only to externals? All the obligations of conformity to the divine ordinances, all the arguments which prove the connection between public worship and the morals of the people, combine to urge adopting some speedy measures, to provide for the public ministry in these churches; if such as have been above recommended should be adopted, and the episcopal succession afterwards obtained, any supposed imperfections of the intermediate ordinations might, if it were judged proper, be supplied without acknowledging their nullity, by a conditional ordination resembling that of conditional baptism in the liturgy; the above was an expedient proposed by Archbishop Tillotson, Bishops Patrick, Stillingfleet and others at the Revolution, and had been actually practised in Ireland by Archbishop Bramhall."[6]

The Connecticut clergy decided that any further delay was impossible. On 25 March, 1783, they met together and chose two of their members as episcopabile, Jeremiah Leaming and Samuel Seabury. The former withdrew because of his age and infirmity, and early in July 1783, Seabury was in London presenting his case. He brought with him certain documents. One of them addressed to the Archbishop of York by the Connecticut clergy indicates the alarm that Dr. White's Case had occasioned: "A further reason, we beg leave to observe, that induces us to take this early and only measure we can devise for this purpose (the obtaining of the historic episcopate), is effectually to prevent the carrying into execution a plan of a very extraordinary nature, lately come to our knowledge, founded and published in Philadelphia, and as we suppose, circulating in the Southern States with design to have it adopted. The plan is, in brief, to constitute a normal ideal Episcopate, by the united suffrages of presbyters and laymen. The singular and peculiar situation of the American Church, the exigence of the case, and the necessity of adopting some speedy and specious remedy, corresponding with the state of affairs in the country, are some of the pleas which are adduced as adequate to give full sanction to the scheme. To what degree such a plan may operate upon the minds of the uninformed, unstable or unprincipled part of the Church, we can at present form no opinion; equally unable are we to conjecture what may be the lengths to which the rage for popular right, as the fountain of all institutions, civil and ecclesiastical, will run; sufficient for us it is, that while we conscientiously reject such a spurious substitute for episcopacy, we also think it our duty to take every step within our power to frustrate its pernicious effects. Thus we are afloat, torn from our anchor, and surrounded with shelves and rocks, on which we are in danger of being dashed to pieces, and have but one port into which we can look, and from whence expect relief".[7]

In the event they were to look into that port in vain.

The Revd. Samuel Seabury was born in 1729 in Groton, Connecticut, where his father was a licensed preacher of the Congregational Church. Two years later, the father was made deacon and priest in the Church of England by the Bishop of London, and was appointed by the Society for the Propagation of the Gospel to the charge of St. James, New London. The son read theology at Yale, and on graduating in 1752 travelled to Britain for the purpose of ordination. Before that, however, he spent a year reading medicine in the University of Edinburgh, and it was not until December 1753 that he was made deacon in Fulham Palace Chapel by John Thomas,the Bishop of Lincoln, acting for the aged Bishop Thomas Sherlock of London. Two days later, he was admitted to the priesthood by Richard Osbaldeston, Bishop of Carlisle. Like his father before him, Seabury was accepted as a missionary priest for the American colonies by the SPG, and returned to his native land to minister in New Brunswick and New York. He had a distinguished record as a parish priest, and in 1777 the University of Oxford conferred upon him an honorary Doctorate of Divinity.

Seabury was a loyalist, a High Churchman and a Tory. He was driven from his charge because of his loyalist writings and sympathies, and spent some weeks in prison in New Haven. In 1777, he was appointed Chaplain to the King's American Regiment, and continued in that capacity until 1783. Shortly afterwards, he was chosen by the clergy of Connecticut as their Bishop-elect.

Two of the documents he brought with him to England in July of that year were addressed to the English Primates. The terms of these documents indicate that the American clergy had a much higher and sounder ideal of the Church in its relation to the State on the one hand, and its spiritual duty to the One "whose kingdom is not of this world" on the other, than the views which were then prevalent in the mother church and in the mother country.[8]

The appeal to the Archbishop of Canterbury (John Moore) admirably puts the case:- "America is now severed from the British Empire; by that separation we cease to be a part of the national church. But, although political changes affect and dissolve our external connection, and cut us off from the powers of the State, yet, we hope, a door still remains open for access to the governors of the Church: and what they might not do for us, without the permission of government, while we are bound as subjects to ask favours, and receive them under the auspices and sanctions, they may, in right of their inherent spiritual powers, grant and exercise in favour of a church planted and nurtured by their hand, and now subjected to other powers … permit us to suggest, with all deference, our firm persuasion that a sense of the sacred Deposit committed by the great Head of the Church to her bishops, is so awfully impressed on your Grace's mind, as not to leave a moment's doubt in us of your being heartily disposed to rescue the American Church from the distress and

danger which now, more than ever, threatened her for want of an Episcopate."
The Connecticut clergy had written for the same purpose in their letter to the Archbishop of York (William Markham): "This part of America is at length dismembered from the British empire, but notwithstanding the dissolution of our civil connection with the parent State, we still hope to retain our religious policy, and primitive and evangelical doctrine and discipline, which at the Reformation were restored and established in the Church of England". And they went on to say that, to complete and perpetuate this policy "an American Episcopate must be secured."[9]

THE ENGLISH APPROACH FAILS

Seabury had arrived in London on 7 July 1783, and lost no time in presenting his case to the two Archbishops and to the Bishop of London, Robert Lowth. He received a cordial welcome from the latter, who gave full approval to the scheme, wished it success, and expressed his willingness to join his brothers of Canterbury and York in granting the candidate episcopal orders. Seabury gathered from the conversation, however, that he would not take the lead in pressing the matter. Lowth mentioned the state oaths required of candidates in the English consecration service for a bishop, suggesting that they might prove an impediment to providing a bishop for a foreign state (as Connecticut now was) but supposing that the king's dispensation could remove the difficulty.

The meeting with the Archbishop of Canterbury did not go so well. The Archbishop was afraid that since a parliamentary act had imposed the oaths, even a royal dispensation could not remove the requirement. All the same he hoped that none of the difficulties that he foresaw would prove insuperable. In the event, the Archbishop was wrong. He and his brother of York eventually gave their opinion that they had no right to send a bishop to Connecticut without the consent of that state (this latter objection apparently originated not with the primates, but with Lord North. Episcopal appointments in England were subject to political control, as they were in every continental monarchy. Would not the governments of the newly independent states wish to exercise the same authority?). There was, too, the fact that there was no guaranteed financial support for the bishop, now that the SPG had withdrawn from the former colonies.

More than a year from Seabury's arrival in England had elapsed before the final answer came from Lambeth Palace. The Archbishop of Canterbury expressed great regret. He had done all he could, but the Cabinet would not allow a Bill to be presented to Parliament to sanction the consecration of an American Bishop. Seabury asked why not. Archbishop Moore listed seven reasons. The Cabinet could not take up the matter until the question of an episcopate for Nova Scotia was settled. They could not act unless the American Congress requested a bishop or, at least acquiesced in the sending of one; Connecticut was just a single state, and even its explicit consent had not been given. The application was only supported by the clergy of Connecticut, there were no lay persons' names on the petition. The Episcopal Laity in the United States were averse to having bishops. The country was not divided into dioceses. Since England had sent no bishop out prior to the War of American Independence, it would look strange if one were despatched now, and might create or exacerbate anti-British feelings.10

Seabury had an interview of an hour-and-a-half with the Archbishop and argued in vain. Once all hopes of an English consecration were at an end, he turned to Scotland.

THE APPROACH TO SCOTLAND

ROBERT KILGOUR
Bishop of Aberdeen 1768-1786 and Primus 1782-1788

The Scottish bishops were to some extent prepared for Seabury's approach. Two years earlier in 1782, The Revd. Dr. George Berkeley, a prebendary of Canterbury and the son of the Bishop of Cloyne, had been in correspondence with The Revd.

John Skinner in Aberdeen. Berkeley had urged the Scottish bishops to take the first opportunity of introducing a Protestant Episcopate into America, asserting that the king would look on such an act with satisfaction. The bishops, after some hesitation, were agreed as to the propriety of what was being suggested, and Skinner wrote: "'Tis not to be doubted but the Bishops of this Church on a proper application, will think it their duty to extend the precious benefit to them."[11]

A more direct and specific approach came to them in November 1783. Seabury had approached a Scottish priest, The Revd. George Bisset, who had served in Newport, Rhode Island, but who was at that time living in London. Before his emigration, Bisset had served as an assistant in a well-known school in Kensington under James Elphinston, the son of a Scottish clergyman, and a minor literary figure. When his former assistant wrote to him about the possibilities of Seabury's consecration at the hands of the Scottish bishops, Elphinston sent on Bissett's letter to a friend in Edinburgh, The Revd. John Allan, minister of St. Paul's Episcopal Chapel in Carubber's Close there.[12]

"You will present, Sir, my just regards to those whom you know me to respect, and will (for I can depend on your zeal as well as prudence) give a definitive answer to the enclosed question which has been put in vain on this side Tweed. An American clergyman whom I have long known, has entreated me to forward the momentous enquiry. The D.D. who is the candidate ready, if encouraged to make the journey to the North, I have never seen. He is an intimate friend of my friend, and respected (I am assured) as known in the country he wishes to bless. His principles I understand to be Apostolic; so in every particular conformable to those of whoever shall have the piety, with the power to promote them."

"The speediest possible answer is hoped from those who alone can give it. Your kind instrumentality may do extended good – and longed for on every account, will be your letter, Sir, by your most obliged and most obedient servant."

Bissett's "momentous enquiry", enclosed in Elphinston's letter, was in these terms:

"Can consecration be obtained in Scotland for an already dignified and well-vouched American clergyman now at London, for the purpose of perpetuating the Episcopal Reformed Church in America, particularly in Connecticut?"

Allan forwarded both letter and enclosure to the Primus, Bishop Kilgour of Aberdeen, who thereupon sent out copies to his brother bishops, asking for their views. The enquiry met with a generally good reception. The Primus was willing to consecrate. Arthur Petrie, Bishop of Moray, would do the same. "The very prospect of the thing rejoices me greatly", he informed Kilgour, "and considering the sacred depositum committed to us, I do not see how we can account to our Great Lord and Master if we neglect such an opportunity of promoting History and enlarging the borders of the Church". The Jacobite Bishop, Charles Rose of Dunblane and Dunkeld, was uneasy. "I have no objection to laying hands upon this American doctor but one, and that is, his having got his orders from the Schismatical Church of England". John Skinner, Coadjutor Bishop of Aberdeen, was initially anxious in case consecrating Seabury should expose the Scottish Episcopalians to danger. There were some grounds for Skinner's anxiety. Active persecution of the Episcopal Church – at its height when Samuel Seabury had previously spent his time in Edinburgh in 1752-53 – had eased well before 1783, once the hopelessness of the Stuart cause had become clear and the reason for it disappeared. Nevertheless, the penal laws were still on the books. Fears that they might be revived exercised an inhibiting influence on the Church – hence the reserve in Bishop Skinner's response to the overture about consecrating a bishop for America.

Skinner's anxiety was relieved by a letter from Dr. George Berkeley, who declared that the king, some Cabinet Ministers and all the bishops except St. Asaph, "and all the learned and respectable clergy in our Church" would rejoice, at least secretly, if Scotland acceded to Seabury's request.13 Berkeley was a close friend of Archbishop Moore, and presumed to be privy to his views on the matter. Skinner communicated this to the Primus, and in December 1783, Kilgour answered Bisset's enquiry in the affirmative. He wrote to The Revd. John Allan that all the bishops except Falconer ("whose declining state may well excuse him from taking any concern") had received with joy the proposal for "conveying Protestant Episcopacy to America and enlarging the borders of the Church of Christ." When they were satisfied as to Seabury's piety, learning and principles, they would readily concur in his consecration.

It is apparent that the Scottish bishops had taken Bisset's note to be a firm proposal, rather than a tentative enquiry dependent upon the outcome of Seabury's transactions with the English bench. In the event, it was not until August of 1784 that the substantive appeal for consecration was made. Seabury wrote to The Revd. Dr. Myles Cooper, formerly President of King's College, New York, and now Minister of New Episcopal Chapel in Edinburgh, who in turn used The Revd. John Allan as intermediary with the College of Bishops. Cooper appended a note to Seabury's letter: "Dr. Cooper presents his most respectful compliments to Bishop Kilgour, and makes leave to acquaint him, that to Dr. Cooper's knowledge, Dr. Seabury is recommended by several worthy clergymen in Connecticut as a person worthy of promotion, and to whom they are willing to submit as a Bishop".

In his letter, Seabury explained the reasons why he had not taken earlier advantage of the Scottish bishops' willingness to accede to his desire for consecration. He set out the circumstances of his failure with the English bishops, and sketched the situation of the Connecticut Episcopal Church. "On this ground it is that I apply to the good Bishops in Scotland, and I hope that I shall not apply in vain. If they consent to impart the Episcopal succession to the Church of Connecticut, they will, I think, do a good work and the blessings of thousands will attend them. And perhaps for this cause, among others, God's Providence has supported them and continued their succession under various and great difficulties – that a free, valid and purely ecclesiastical Episcopacy may from them pass into the Western World."14

Allan sent the letter on to the Primus, who in turn wrote to Petrie: "As Dr. Seabury had been so long silent, I reckoned the Affair had been dropped, but as he accounts for his Conduct in so open and candid a manner I still think we should not deny his Request." Presuming that his three colleagues would agree with this (Bishop Falconer had recently died) Kilgour wrote a reply to Allan: "I have the pleasure to inform you that we are still willing to comply with his (Seabury's) proposal: to cloath him with the Episcopal character, and thereby convey to the Western World the blessing of a free, valid and purely ecclesiastical Episcopacy; not doubting that he will so agree with us in Doctrine and Discipline, as that he and the Church under his charge in Connecticut, will hold communion with us and the Church here on Catholic and Primitive principles; and so that the members of both may with freedom communicate together in all the Offices of Religion." Kilgour went on to hope that Dr. Seabury would let him know as soon as possible the date of his arrival in Scotland, so that the date for the consecration could be fixed. He concluded: "May God grant us a happy meeting, and direct all to the honour and glory of His name and to the good of his Church."15

Seabury, on being apprised of the bishops' decision, set out for Scotland on the 24 October 1784. He travelled via Edinburgh where he renewed his acquaintance with Myles Cooper, arriving in Aberdeen on the evening of 5 November. The following morning he called on the Primus, and the date of the consecration was fixed of the 14 November. During the intervening days he made contact with Arthur Petrie of Moray and John Skinner of Aberdeen, who would be the co-consecrators with Robert Kilgour, the Primus.

Chapter XIII
CONSECRATION OF SAMUEL SEABURY
CONSECRATION AND CONCORDAT

JOHN SKINNER
Bishop of Aberdeen 1786-1816 and Primus 1788-1816

The preparations for Seabury's consecration on the 14 November 1784 were made with meticulous care. On the day before the service, the three bishops – Kilgour, Petrie and Skinner – met with the candidate and examined his references and testimonials. These were all recorded in the Register of the Episcopal Synod, together with details of the circumstances attending his application to the Scottish

Bishops. Having satisfied themselves that the Bishop-elect was "a man of blameless conduct, orthodox in the faith, apt to teach, fit to govern, and having a good report as well of those who are without as of those within the Church", as required by the Code of Canons, they were ready to proceed with the consecration.1

The service took place on the Sunday in a large upper room of Skinner's house in Long Acre, Aberdeen, beginning with Morning Prayer followed by a celebration of the Holy Communion. The sermon was preached by Skinner, taking as his text the apostolic commission from Matthew 28, verses 18 to 20. It was a typical exposition of the High Church doctrine of episcopal succession, containing also an attack upon Erastian principles with its reference to the Church of England "having more regard to the Acts of Parliament than to the Acts of the Apostles."2 That reference did not please English friends of the Scottish Church who believed that it reflected unfairly on their own bishops. The sermon was not without its critics too, within the Church in Scotland, notably The Revd. George Gleig, at that time Episcopal Minister at Stirling, and later Bishop of Brechin and Primus. He had, he said, found Skinner's sermon in unity of subject and in perspicacity of thought "so miserably deficient that although I have read it again and again with the closest attention, I can only hazard a probable conjecture as to what are the main doctrines its author means to inculcate."3

The sermon was followed by the actual consecration, with the three bishops laying their hands on Seabury. The folio Prayer Book from which the consecrators read, was held by a young priest from Stonehaven, The Revd. Alexander Jolly. In due course, Jolly was to become Bishop of Moray, and himself take part in another notable consecration – that of Dr. Matthew Luscombe as Missionary Bishop of the Scottish Episcopal Church. After the imposition of hands, the eucharistic liturgy continued, and the service ended with the newly consecrated bishop giving the blessing. The American Episcopate had begun. The same day, in the late afternoon, Bishop Seabury preached at Evening Prayer in Skinner's Long Acre Chapel, surprising the congregation with the earnest manner of his delivery, and the use of a white handkerchief to emphasise points in his sermon. Unfortunately, no record of that sermon is known to exist.

On the Monday, the four bishops met together again in Bishop Skinner's house. They were engaged upon a work that the Primus had considered to be a most desirable, if not essential, part of the whole proceedings. In a note to Skinner on 2 October 1784, when the bishops had agreed in principle to Seabury's consecration, Kilgour had written: "Will it not be proper that there be a concordat, some bond of union drawn upon Catholick principles, and subscribed by Dr. Seabury and us, and likewise a letter written and sent by him to the Clergy in Connecticut? I think by the law passed by the Congress in their favour they will have privileges beyond any part of the Christian Church I know of and free from all Erastian shackles, and I hope they will think themselves happy in having a valid, free and purely Ecclesiastical

Episcopacy conveyed to them by us, which they could have had nowhere else. And it gives me pleasure to think that God is likely to make us the instruments of so great a blessing and extending the Kingdom of our Lord to these parts – where, if for the sins of this nation, He should let it fail here, may be found and flourish, which God grant it ever may."

"This Concordat and letter I hope you will take into consideration and make a scroll of, that we may have as little to do as possible when it please God we meet."4

Skinner did his work well, and at the meeting on the Monday, all was ready for consideration by the four bishops. The Concordat and the Letter were studied and agreed without alteration. The Concordat is set out here because it set a pattern for the mutual responsibility and interdependence which was to become the watchword of the Anglican Communion.

After invoking the holy and undivided Trinity, the preamble to the Concordat begins:

"The wise and gracious Providence of the merciful God, having put it into the hearts of the Christians of the Episcopal persuasion in Connecticut and North America, to desire that the Blessings of a free, valid and purely Ecclesiastical Episcopacy might be communicated to them, and of a church regularly found in that part of the western world upon the most ancient and primitive Model …"

The reference to a free, valid and purely Ecclesiastical Episcopacy represents the pattern of the Anglican Communion as it has developed outside England, where episcopacy to this day still has elements of a position and responsibilities which could not truly be called "purely Ecclesiastical". The Concordat went on to refer to the choice of Samuel Seabury, and to the belief that this was only the beginning of work in America. "Animated with this pious hope, and earnestly desirous to establish a bond of peace and Holy Communion between the two Churches, " the bishops set out seven Articles upon which they were agreed:

1. "They agree in thankfully receiving, and humbly and heartily embracing the whole Doctrine of the Gospel, as revealed and set forth in the holy Scriptures: and it is their earnest and united Desire to maintain the Analogy of the common Faith once delivered to the Saints, and happily preserved in the Church of Christ, through his divine power and protection, who promised that the gates of Hell should never prevail against it."

2. "They agree in believing this Church to be the mystical Body of Christ, of which he alone is the Head, and Supreme Governor, and that under him, the chief Minister or Managers of the affairs of this spiritual society, are those called bishops, whose exercise of their sacred office being independent of all Lay powers, it follows of consequence that their spiritual Authority, and Jurisdiction cannot be affected by any Lay-Deprivation."

3. "They agree in declaring that the Episcopal Church in Connecticut is to be in full communion with the Episcopal Church in Scotland, it being their sincere

Resolution to put matters in such a footing that the Members of both Churches may with freedom and safety communicate with either, when their Occasions call them from the one country to the other."

4. "With a view to the salutary purpose mentioned in the preceding Articles, they agree in desiring that there may be as near a Conformity in Worship and Discipline established between the two Churches, as is consistent with the different Circumstances and Customs of Nations, and in order to avoid any bad Effects that might otherwise arise from political Differences, they hereby express their earnest wish and firm Intention to observe such prudent Generality in their public Prayers, with respect to these points, as shall appear most agreeable to Apostolic Rules, and the true practice of the primitive Church."

5. "As the Celebration of the Holy Eucharist, or the Administration of the Sacrament of the Body and Blood of Christ, is the principal Bond of Union among Christians as well as the most Solemn Act of Worship in the Christian Church, the bishops aforesaid agree in desiring that there may be as little Variance here as possible. And tho' the Scottish Bishops are very far from prescribing to their Brethren in this matter, they cannot help ardently wishing that Bishop Seabury would endeavour all he can consistently with peace and prudence, to make the Celebration of this venerable Mystery conformable to the most primitive Doctrine and practice in that respect: Which is the pattern the Church of Scotland has copied after in her Communion Office, and which it has been the wish of some of the most eminent Divines of the Church of England that she had more closely followed than she seems to have done since she gave up her first reformed Liturgy used in the Reign of King Edward VI, between which and the form used in the Church of Scotland there is no Difference in any point, which the primitive Church reckoned essential to the right Ministration of the holy Eucharist. In this capital Article therefore of the Eucharistic Service in which the Scottish Bishops so earnestly wish for as much Unity as possible, Bishop Seabury also agreed to take a serious View of the Communion Office recommended by them, and if found agreeable to the genuine Standards of Antiquity, to give his Sanction to it, and by gentle methods of Argument and persuasion, to endeavour, as they have done, to introduce it by degrees into practice without the Compulsion of Authority on the one side, or the prejudice of former Custom on the other."

6. "It is also hereby agreed and resolved upon for the better answering the purposes of this Concordat, that a brotherly fellowship be hence-forth maintained between the Episcopal Churches in Scotland and Connecticut, and such a mutual Intercourse of Ecclesiastical correspondence carried on, when Opportunity offers, or necessity requires as may tend to the Support, and Edification of both Churches."

7. "The Bishops aforesaid do hereby jointly declare, in the most solemn manner, that in the whole of this Transaction they have nothing else in view, but the Glory of God, and the Good of his Church; and being thus pure and upright in their intentions, they cannot but hope that all whom it may concern, will put the most

fair and candid construction on their Conduct, and take no offence at their feeble but sincere Endeavours to promote what they believe to be the Cause of Truth, and of the common Salvation."5

THE EPISCOPATE BEGINS

On the Thursday after Seabury's Consecration, Bishop Skinner wrote to The Revd. Dr. George Berkeley, who had first raised the question of an American episcopate with him two years earlier:- "I have the pleasure to acquaint you that Dr. Seabury, the worthy clergyman so amply recommended from Connecticut, was consecrated in my Chapel last Lord's Day ... As I know this is a matter which you have very much at heart I have taken the liberty of troubling you with a copy of the Articles of Union which our Church has entered into with the rising church in Connecticut, and of the Letter which we have written to the Episcopal clergy there, requesting their compliance with these Articles, as conductive to the support and edification of those Churches. This, you may believe, is the only end we have in view, by the part we have acted in this affair, and we shall be happy to think that it meets with your approbation. That of your Bps. perhaps, we are not entitled to expect – yet we will flatter ourselves that they will not think the worse of us for taking up the good work which they, it seems, by reason of their State connection were obliged to leave to our management."6

Seabury stayed with Skinner for several days after the signing of the Concordat, and then began his way back to London, taking with him his Latin Letter of Orders as a Bishop, the attested copies of the Scottish succession of Bishops since 1688, the Concordat and the Letter from the Scottish bishops. On the 24 November he was in Dundee with The Revd. John Strachan (later Bishop of Brechin 1787 – 1810). Three days later he reached Edinburgh where his hosts were The Revd. John Allan of St. Paul's Chapel and William Abernethy Drummond (later successively the Bishop of Brechin, 1787, of Edinburgh 1787 – 1805 and of Glasgow 1805 – 1809).
After the warmth of his reception in Scotland, the ecclesiastical atmosphere in England was very cold by contrast. The Archbishops of Canterbury and York were reported to be much displeased by what had transpired, and it was not until the eve of his departure back to America that Seabury called on them. Both Archbishops then received him warmly enough. They regretted that he had proceeded as he had done, and hoped that none of the consequences that they dreaded would occur. The Establishment, including the Society for the Propagation of the Gospel, studiously avoided addressing him as Bishop, using only his academic title of Doctor.7
The journey to Connecticut was slow and it was not until the 2nd August 1785 that the new Bishop was installed in the Church of Middletown and seated on an

improvised cathedra. An address of welcome was read and Seabury thanked the clergy. They then knelt for the episcopal blessing before returning to their pews. Connecticut had received its bishop.

On the 16 September 1785, the clergy of what was now the Diocese of Connecticut addressed a letter to the Bishops of the Scottish Episcopal Church:-"Reverend Fathers, The pastoral letter which your Christian attention excited you to address to us from Aberdeen on November 15 1784 was duly delivered to us by the Rt. Rev. Bishop Seabury and excited in us the warmest sentiments, gratitude and esteem. We should much earlier have made our acknowledgements had not our dispersed situation made the difficulty of our meeting together so very great; and the multiplicity of business absolutely necessary to be immediately dispatched so entirely engrossed our time at our first meeting at Middletown as to render it then impracticable.

We never had the least doubt of the validity or regularity of the succession of the Scottish Bishops & as we never desired any other Bps In this Country than than upon the principles of the primitive Apostolical Church, we should from the very first have been as much pleased with a Bp from Scotland as from England.

But our connection with the English Church and the kind support that most of our clergy received from the Society for the Propagation of the Gospel naturally led us to renew our application to that Church, when we found ourselves separated from the British Government by the late peace.

We are utterly at a loss to account for the backwardness of the British Church Government to send Bishops to this Country which has long & earnestly been requested, and we do think that their refusal to consecrate Dr. Seabury under the circumstances that we applied for it, was utterly inconsistent with sound policy and Christian principles.

Greatly then are we indebted to you Venerable Fathers for your kind & Christian interposition, and wo do heartily thank God that he did of his mercy put it into your hearts to consider & relieve our necessity.

We also greatly revere and acknowledge the readiness with which you gratified our ardent wishes to have a Bp to complete our Religious Establishment. We receive it as the gift of God himself through your hands. And though much is to be done to collect and regulate a scattered & till now, unorganized Church, yet we hope through patience, diligence and propriety of Conduct, by God's Blessing, in due time to accomplish it & make the Church of Connecticut a fair and fruitful Branch of the Church Universal.

Our utmost exertions shall be joined with those of our Bp to preserve the unity of the Faith, Doctrine, Discipline & Uniformity of Worship with the Church from which we derive our Episcopacy & with which it will be our praise and happiness to keep up the most intimate intercourse and Communion.

Commending ourselves & our Church to your prayers & Benediction, we are Rt. Reverend Venerable Fathers,

Your most dutiful Sons & servants,
Signed on behalf of the whole by
Abraham Jarvis, Secretary
Of the Convocation of the Episcopal Clergy in Connecticut."[8]

CONSECRATION OF SAMUEL SEABURY
Aberdeen 14 November 1748 84

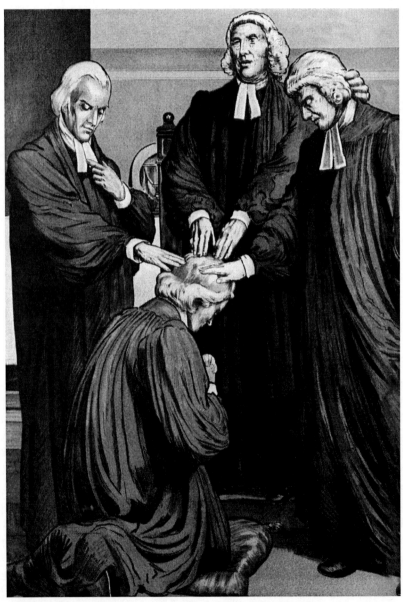

Chapter XIV
SEABURY AND AFTER
TRIUMPH AND TRIBULATIONS

Within Connecticut, Seabury began at once to review and reorganise the churches of his diocese. By December 15 of the year of his installation, he had ordained twelve priests from six states. Seven years later, he reported having travelled more than six thousand miles, confirmed more than ten thousand candidates, and ordained thirty priests and eight deacons – probably almost the equivalent of the size of the ministry and membership of the Scottish Episcopal Church at the time of his consecration. He succeeded, too, by gentle persuasion, in fulfilling the terms of Article 5 of the Concordat, leaving the American Episcopal Church with the Scottish Liturgy as the pattern of its eucharistic worship.1

The tradition of the Church Catholic requires for a regular consecration the laying on of hands by three bishops. There was obviously a need for more bishops if the American Church was to become independent and capable of self-perpetuation. An Act of Parliament had been passed in 1784 to "impower the Bishop of London for the time being, or any other bishop to be by him appointed, to admit to the order of deacon or priest persons being subjects or citizens out of his Majesty's dominions, without requiring them to take the oath of allegiance as appointed by law."2 No doubt spurred on by the Seabury consecration, under a later Act of 1786, the English primates were empowered to consecrate persons who were subjects or citizens of countries outside the King's dominions.3 Already in anticipation of this possibility; the American conventions had chosen three priests as bishops-designate. They were William White, for Pennsylvania, Samuel Provoost, for New York and David Griffith for Virginia. It is indicative of the poverty of the American Church at the time, that the passage money could not be found for the latter's voyage to England. In the event, only White and Provoost were consecrated in Lambeth Palace Chapel on Sunday, 4 February, 1787, by the two Archbishops assisted by the Bishops of Bath and Wells and of Peterborough.4

There were now three bishops in the American Church, two in the English succession and Seabury in the Scottish; sufficient to consecrate other bishops. But the Bishops of Pennsylvania and of New York refused to join with the Bishop of Connecticut in consecrating Dr. Griffith of Virginia and The Revd. Edward Bass, a candidate put forward by Massachusetts.5 They gave as a reason for their refusal, their obligation to the Bishops of the Church of England who had consecrated them. It became apparent that the English Primates had required an understanding that any consecration in America should not take place with Bishop Seabury as the third consecrator. This would have to wait for a third priest to go to Lambeth to receive English episcopal orders so that the American Church would derive its bishops entirely from the Church of England. Bishop White wrote:

"I will be very explicit with you on the questions you put with regard to an Union with Bishop Seabury and the Consecration of Dr. Griffith. On the one hand, considering it was presumed a third was to go over to England, that the institutions of the Church of that Country required three to join in the Consecration and that the political situation of the English Prelates prevents their official knowledge of Dr. Seabury as a Bishop, I am apprehensive it may seem a Breach of Faith towards them, if not an intended Deception in us, were we to consecrate without the usual Number, and those all under the English succession …"

Bishop Provoost was even more explicit. Writing to Bishop White, he replied "As to what you style an implied engagement to the English Bishops, I look upon it in regard to myself as a positive one."[6]

It was not until 1789 that The Revd. James Madison, President of William and Mary College, was consecrated at Lambeth as the first Bishop of Virginia. In a letter to William White in December 1790, Madison conveyed the Archbishop of Canterbury's maintained opinion on consecrations in America: "A few days before I left, the Archbishop requested a particular Interview with me. He said he wish'd to express his Hopes, and also to recommend to our Church, that, in such consecrations as might take place in America, the persons who had received their Powers from the Church of England would alone be concerned. He spoke with great delicacy of Dr. Seabury, but thought it more advisable that the Line of Bishops should be passed down from those who had received their Commission from the same source."[7] The fundamental problem was that if White and Provoost had joined with Seabury in consecrating a fourth bishop, it would have been tantamount to recognising the validity of the Scots succession, whose powers of ordination were not acknowledged by Parliament.

In due course, in September 1792, all four bishops – Seabury, White, Provoost and Madison – joined together in consecrating The Revd. Thomas John Claggett as first Bishop of Maryland. But this was not until White had solemnly pledged that he would take no part in Claggett's elevation if the other bishops refused Seabury's assistance.[8] Of this sorry episode on the part of the English Establishment, Dr. William Jones Seabury has this verdict:

"Through Bishop Claggett every Bishop since consecrated in the American Episcopate traces his line of Episcopal succession; and thus every one of those Bishops derives his Episcopate from the Scottish line as well as from the English line.

"So God overruled the malice of those Bishops who, having through their connection with the State been deprived of the opportunity of being the first to transmit the Apostolic succession to the Western World, sought to secure the credit of an action which they had been afraid to perform, by depreciating an Episcopacy which they knew to be as valid as their own. And so the act of the Scottish Bishops in consecrating a Bishop for Connecticut, has, in the Providence of God, stamped an impress on the American Episcopate which will last as long as the power of the American succession to perpetuate itself shall endure.

"Short sighted indeed was that prejudice which made the English Bishops, and those whom they consecrated for us in 1787, cast doubtful glances upon the consecration of 1784, and led them to such scrupulous circumspection lest they should seem to permit the American succession to depend for the completion of its canonical number of consecrators upon the Bishop of Connecticut. And much reason have we to be thankful that the life of that Bishop was preserved until their scrupulous, though dangerous, nicety was satisfied; for had he died before the three Bishops consecrated in England were ready to perform their first consecration in this Country, we should indeed have had the Episcopal succession, but we should have been deprived of the happiness of tracing it through those who had lived to show the world the possibility of maintaining the succession without the help of the Establishment, and in spite of tyrannical efforts to stamp it out of existence. Nor should we have had the privilege of showing the concentration of several lines sometime separated, but now in our succession united; and thereby symbolising the true purpose and notion of the Episcopate as the Divinely appointed centre of unity in the Church of Christ."[9]

There was an ironical twist to all this. The Act under which White, Provoost and Madison had been consecrated (26 Geo III C35) contained this ominous clause:-

"III, Provided also, and be it hereby declared, that no Person or Persons consecrated to the Office of Bishop in the manner aforesaid, nor any Person or Persons admitted to the Order of Deacon or Priest by any Bishop or Bishops so consecrated, or by the Successor or Successors of any Bishop or Bishops so consecrated, shall be thereby enabled to exercise his or their respective Office or Offices within His Majesty's Dominions."

As a result of this clause, American bishops and clergy were treated in England as visiting laymen permitted neither to officiate nor preach. The Scots, having entered into full communion through their concordat with Bishop Seabury, ignored the Act. It was not until 1842, and then through the efforts of the Bishop of Glasgow, that the disabling effect of the Act of 1786 was partially lifted. As Canon Herklots remarks:

"In face of such hindrances, the Anglican Communion was to struggle into being … it was in the small church north of the Border that they understood far better the meaning of mutual responsibility and interdependence in the Body of Christ".[10]

Samuel Seabury died on the 25 February 1796. He left a lasting impression on the corpus of theology of the American Church, not least through the Scottish Catechism which he introduced to Connecticut and Rhode Island, and in the influence of the Scottish Communion Office of 1764 on the American Liturgy.

His body lies beneath an altar-tomb in the Church of St. James', New London. Above it, is a brass plate inscribed in Latin:-

"Under the pavement of this altar, as in the final place of rest until the great Day of Judgement, now repose the mortal remains of the Right Reverend Bishop Samuel Seabury, Doctor of Divinity of the University of Oxford, who first brought from Scotland into the Anglo-American Republic of the New World, the Apostolic Succession, the 14 November 1784."

THE UNITED STATES

By the beginning of the nineteenth century, seven bishops presided in America over their several sees. Samuel Seabury's successor had been consecrated for Connecticut. There were diocesan bishops, too, in Maryland, Pennsylvania, Massachusetts, New York, Virginia and South Carolina. Three of the seven were in English Episcopal orders, the rest had been consecrated on American soil. The Protestant Episcopal Church of the United States of America had become an independent, autonomous church. There were now the three separate churches in England, Scotland and America, which were eventually to grow into the Anglican Communion.

It could not, however, properly be said that the Scottish and American Episcopal Churches were then in full, or even in limited, communion with the Church of England. Their clergy were precluded by statute from holding preferment or officiating in churches under the jurisdiction of the Archbishop of Canterbury. Indeed, even the sacraments administered by Scots and American clergy were not legally registerable. No such difficulties existed between Scotland and America, so that paradoxically it might fairly be said that the Anglican Communion had its beginnings outside and despite the Church of England.

Independence and autonomy for the American Episcopal Church meant that there was no longer any need for ordinands to travel three thousand miles across the Atlantic to obtain the consent of "a cross old man at Canterbury". The last American Bishop to be consecrated in Lambeth Palace Chapel was James Madison in 1790. From then onwards, most of the clergy were drawn from native-born citizens of the United States, like Dr. Thomas Claggett of Maryland, the first bishop consecrated on American soil.

Claggett combined the duties of running a parish with the oversight of his diocese. This was to remain the normal pattern of American Episcopal ministry for some years. It followed the practice of the Scottish Episcopal Church whose bishops had invariably also been incumbents. Alexander Penrose Forbes, for example, was both Bishop of Brechin and incumbent of St. Paul's, Dundee from his consecration in 1847 until his death in 1874, when the practice finally ceased. Bishops of the Church of England had never had this dual responsibility of office.[11]

"For twenty years, Bishop Claggett had been overburdened by the united weight of those cares which belong to a laborious parish priest and those which press upon a faithful bishop ... Worn out by such labours yet unwilling wholly to desert his post, Bishop Claggett, after twenty years of service, applied in 1812 for a suffragan to share his task".

He received permission for this on the understanding that the presbyter so elected by the Maryland Diocesan Synod would have the right to succeed him. In this, he was following the peculiarly Scottish practice (in Anglicanism at least) of appointing co-adjutor bishops with automatic right of succession. This is a procedure still permitted in terms of the American canons, and which was also possible in Scotland until the regulations were finally rescinded in 1984. The priest who was eventually elected as Claggett's successor was a Scot, The Revd. James Kemp.

Kemp was born in 1764 in the village of Keith Hall in Aberdeenshire. His parents were devout Presbyterians who brought their son up in that Church. After attending the local school, he went on to Marischal College in the University of Aberdeen where he graduated Master of Arts in 1786 He had, in the meantime, become an Episcopalian. Bishop Michael Russell's account of Kemp's boyhood says that when first permitted to attend episcopalian worship "he was wont to be led blindfold to the house of prayer, lest he should afterwards prove a traitor and expose his fellow-worshippers to the severe enactments of a persecuting code. Probably this attachment to the Church led to his emigrating to America".

For a couple of years after his arrival in the United States, the young graduate acted as tutor to a family in Eastern Maryland. He began reading for holy orders under the supervision of The Revd. John Bowie, rector of the local episcopal church in Great Choptank, and in 1789 was made deacon and priest by William White, the Bishop of Pennsylvania, there being no diocese of Maryland at that time. In due course he succeeded Bowie as rector of the parish, was made a Doctor of Divinity by Columbia College in 1802, and eleven years later became associate rector of St. Paul's, Baltimore, the largest congregation in the state.

It was from here that Kemp was elected as suffragan to Thomas Claggett, who had become the first bishop of the newly-formed diocese of Maryland in 1792. Kemp's election was not without difficulty, reflecting something of the internal tensions of the diocese.

An early American church historian described the situation of the diocese at the time of the election. "Maryland was at this time under the charge of Bishop Claggett, a mild and courteous ruler, and a zealous Christian minister, but wanting somewhat of that habitual firmness which was needful to give tone to his episcopate. His flock was in a languishing condition: it was, moreover sorely harassed by internal disputes; parties ran high within it, and it seemed as if the unity of the spirit had departed from the land. Bishop Claggett could scarcely repress the feuds which were rife among his clergy; and as soon as opportunity allowed, they broke out in visible dissentions."

Kemp's election provided just such an opportunity, and became the occasion of a schism in the form of "The Evangelical Episcopal Church" under the leadership of one of the Maryland clergy, The Revd. Daniel Dashiell.

The schism was short-lived and never involved more than four or five clergymen. Nevertheless, it posed a severe threat to the young diocese. Kemp finally succeeded Claggett as diocesan in 1816, and by firmness, tact and modernisation, was able to heal the schism. His episcopate came at a critical time for Maryland, and in the eleven years until his death in 1827, his leadership enabled the diocese to share in the general revival of the church which had begun under Bishop John Hobart in New York and James Madison in Virginia.[12]

Kemp was the last of a long line of Scots who had made a direct contribution to the life of American episcopalianism. He was in the mould of Blair and Keith, Muirson, Honyman, Inglis and Stuart, with many other Scottish clergy whose ministry had been of incalculable value in helping to lay the foundations of the Protestant Episcopal Church of the United States of America.

BIBLIOGRAPHY

UNPUBLISHED SOURCES
Register of Consecrations, Scottish Episcopal Church
West Register House, Edinburgh
Minutes of the College of Bishops of the Scottish Episcopal Church
Lambeth Palace, London
Register of Consecrations, Lambeth Palace Chapel
Fulham Manuscripts – Virginia Box
Rhodes House Library, Oxford
Archives of the Society for the Propagation of the Gospel in Foreign Parts
Synod Minutes of the Diocese of St. Andrews, Dunkeld and Dunblane

PERIODICALS, NEWSPAPERS ETC.
Scottish Guardian
Scottish Standard Bearer
Society for the Propagation of the Gospel – Journals
Historical Magazine of the Protestant Episcopal Church

COLLECTIONS, DIRECTORIES ETC.
Year Books of the Scottish Episcopal Church
Dictionary of National Biography
Dictionary of American Biography
Scottish Episcopal Clergy 1689-2000
Oxford Dictionary of the Christian Church

PUBLISHED SOURCES
J. Anderson. The Black Book of Kincardineshire. Stonehaven 1843
J. S. M. Anderson. History of the Colonial Church. London 1876
O. Anderson. 400 Years. Cincinnati 1997
E. E. Beardsley. Life and Correspondence of Bishop Seabury. Boston 1882
J. Bramhall. Works (3 volumes). Oxford 1857
W. R. Brock. Scotus Americanus. Edinburgh 1982
G. M. Brydon. Virginia's Mother Church. Richmond 1945
N. R. Burr. The Anglican Church in New Jersey. Philadelphia 1954
A. Carlyle. Autobiography. London 1860
E. Carpenter. The Protestant Bishop. London 1956
T. B. Chandler. Life of Samuel Johnson D.D. London 1824
G. R. Cragg. Puritanism in the Period of the Great Persecution 1660-1668. Cambridge 1951
A. L. Cross. The Anglican Episcopate in the American Colonies. London 1902
F. L. Deane. Sermon preached in St. Mary's Cathedral, Edinburgh 1944. Edinburgh 1957

G. Donaldson. Scottish Church History. Edinburgh 1985
R. E. Fall. The Diary of Robert Rose, Verona. Virginia 1977
G. H. Forbes. Bishop Rattray's Works. New Pitsligo 1854
R. W. Foskett. Some Scottish Links with the American Episcopal Church. Edinburgh 1962
J. A. Garraty. The American Nation. New York 1991
F. Goldie. A Short History of the Scottish Episcopal Church. Edinburgh 1976
H. Henson. The National Church. London 1908
H. G. Herklots. Frontiers of the Church. London 1961
H. G. Herklots. The Church of England in America. London 1966
G. M. Hills. History of the Church in Burlington, New Jersey. Trenton 1885
D. L. Holmes. A Brief History of the Episcopal Church. Valley Forge 1993
W. F. Hook. The Peculiar Character of the Church of England, independently of its connection with the State. London 1822
G. Keith. Journal. London 1706
E. W. Kemp. Introduction to the Canon Law of the Church of England. London 1957
J. Ker. Memoirs of John Ker of Kersland. Edinburgh 1726
W. B. Lee. Colonial Churches in Virginia. Richmond 1907
M. Lochhead. Episcopal Scotland in the Nineteenth Century. London 1966
L. E. Luscombe. A Seminary of Learning. Edinburgh 1996
J. W. Lydekker. Life and Letters of Charles Inglis. London 1936
J. W. Lydekker. The Faithful Mohawks. Cambridge 1938
S. D. McConnell. The English Church in the Colonies. London 1891
J. McVicker. The Early Life and Professional Years of Bishop Hobart. Oxford 1838
H. T. Malone. The Episcopal Church in Georgia 1733-1957. Atlanta 1957
C. Mampoteng. New England Clergy in the American Revolution. New Brunswick 1940
B. L. Manning. The Protestant Dissenting Deputies. Cambridge 1952
M. W. Manross. A History of the American Episcopal Church. New York 1959
A. P. Middleton. Anglican Maryland 1692-1792. Virginia Beach 1992
J. R. H. Moorman. History of the Church of England. London 1954
J. D. Mowat. Bishop A. P. Forbes. Edinburgh 1925
S. Neill. Anglicanism. London 1951
J. K. Nelson. A Blessed Company. Chapel Hill, Virginia 2002
C. F. Pascoe. Two Hundred Years of the SPG (2 Volumes). London 1901
E. L. Pennington. Commissary Blair. Philadelphia 1936
E. L. Pennington. Apostle of New Jersey. Philadelphia 1938
W. S. Perry. The American Episcopal Church. Boston 1885
Seabury Centenary. Connecticut Papers. Connecticut 1885
W. J. Seabury. Memoir of Bishop Seabury. New York 1908
W. Scott. Guy Mannering. London
J. H. Shepherd. Introduction to the History of The Church in Scotland. London 1906
John Skinner. Ecclesiastical History of Scotland. London 1788

J. Skinner. The Nature and Extent of the Apostolical Commission. Aberdeen 1785
W. A. Spooner. Bishop Butler. London 1901
B. E. Steiner. Samuel Seabury. Ohio 1971
W. R. W. Stephens. Life and Letters of W. F. Hook (2 Volumes). London 1880
T. Stephen. History of the Church of Scotland. London 1845
S. W. Sykes (Ed). Authority in the Anglican Communion. Toronto 1987
E. W. Thomson. Life of Thomas Bray. London 1954
H. P. Thompson. Into All Lands. London 1951
H. R. Trevor-Roper. Archbishop Laud. London 1940
M. B. Turner. Colonial Churches in Virginia. Richmond 1908
W. White. The Case of the Episcopal Church in the United States. Philadelphia 1782 reprinted 1954
J. Whitehead. Life of The Revd. Charles Wesley. London 1893
S. Wilberforce. A History of the Protestant Episcopal Church in America. London 1844
John F. Woolverton. Colonial Anglicanism in North America. Detroit 1984

NOTES

I INTRODUCTION

1   D. L. Holmes. A Brief History of the Episcopal Church.
       (Pennsylvania 1993)
       J. F. Woolverton. Colonial Anglicanism in North America. (Detroit
       1984) 271
2   J. K. Nelson. A Blessed Company. (Chapel Hill N.C. 2002) 370
       (Note 2 has an analysis of the known birthplace of fifty-six per cent of
       Colonial Clergy – showing twenty-eight per cent as Scottish)

II CHURCH AND STATE IN SCOTLAND

1   G. Donaldson. Scottish Church History. (Edinburgh 1985) 195
2   ibid 211
3   J. Anderson. The Black Book of Kincardineshire. (Stonehaven 1843) 53-
       54
4   A. Carlyle. Autobiography (London 1860) 249
5   D. Bertie. Scottish Episcopal Clergy 1689-2000. (Edinburgh 2000) 649
6   19 Geo 11 / Cap 38, 21 Geo 11 / Cap 34
7   J. Skinner. Ecclesiastical History of Scotland. (London 1788) 630-63
8   W. Scott. Guy Mannering. (London) 217
9   F. L. Deane. Sermon preached in St. Mary's Cathedral, Edinburgh.
       9 May 1944 (Edinburgh 1957)

10   J. H. Shepherd. Introduction to the History of the Church in Scotland.
      (London 1906) 174
11   Scottish Episcopal Church Year Book 1888
12   Minutes of the Synod of the Diocese of St. Andrews, Dunkeld and
      Dunblane 1888
13   T. Stephen. History of the Church of Scotland. (London 1845) Cap 46
14   Scottish Guardian 1867
15   S. W. Sykes (Ed). Authority in the Anglican Communion. (Toronto 1987)
      Essay by P. H. Thomas. 123
16   Acts of the Parliament of Scotland. XI 402 Cap 6
17   Code of Canons of the Episcopal Church in Scotland. 1743, 1811, 1828,
      1863
18   W. R. W. Stephens. Life and Letters of W. F. Hook (2 Volumes). London
      1880 i 143
19   L. E. Luscombe. A Seminary of Learning. (Edinburgh 1986) passim
20   E. W. Kemp. An Introduction to the Canon Law of the Church of England.
      (London 1957) 6966
21   G. H. Forbes Bishop Rattray's Works (New Pitsligo 1854) 850
22   S. W. Sykes (Ed) op.cit Essay by Louis Weil 63
23   Fulham MSS. Virginia. Box iii f 187
24   F. Goldie. A Short History of the Episcopal Church in Scotland.
      (Edinburgh 1976) 102

III CHURCH AND STATE IN COLONIAL AMERICA

1   The Treaty of Paris 1783
2   E. Goodwin and Others. Colonial Churches in the Original Colony of
      Virginia.
      (Richmond, Virginia 1908) 1-33
3   H. G. G. Herklots. The Church of England and the American Episcopal
      Church.
      (London 1966) Cap iii
4   D. L. Holmes. op. cit. 30
5   A. P. Middleton. Anglican Maryland 1692-1792. (Philadelphia 1954) 9-30
6   J. A. Garraty. The American Nation. (New York 1991) 24
7   H. T. Malone. The Episcopal Church in Georgia. 1733-1957 (Atlanta
      1960) Cap I
8   C. F. Pascoe. Two Hundred Years of the Society for the Propagation of the
      Gospel.
      (London 1901) The statistics are printed in the preamble to the Reports on
      each Colony

9   E. Carpenter. The Protestant Bishop. (London 1956) 253
10   E. Carpenter. op.cit. 267
11   E. L. Perrington. Apostle of New Jersey – John Talbot. (Philadelphia 1938) passim
12   S. Neill. Anglicanism. (London 1958) 223

IV THE SCOTTISH COMMISSARIES

1   G. M. Brydon. Virginia's Mother Church. (Richmond 1945)
2   E. Carpenter. op.cit. 263
3   Fulham MSS. Virginia Box 1 fo 77
4   E. L. Pennington. Commissary Blair. (Philadelphia 1936) 10
5   S. D. McConnell. The English Church in the Colonies. (London 1891) 113
6   D. L. Holmes. op.cit. 22
7   Fulham MSS. Virginia. Box iii fo 59
8   Fulham MSS. Virginia. Box iii fo 187
9   H. G. Herklots. op.cit. 40
10   Tyler. History of American Literature. (1879) quoted by Carpenter in The Protestant Bishop ii 260
11   E. L. Pennington. Historical Magazine of the Protestant Episcopal Church.
        (New York March 1934) 48
12   Fulham MSS. South Carolina. Box 252
13   E. L. Pennington. op. cit. 52-3
14   Fulham MSS. North Carolina, South Carolina and Georgia
15   E. L. Pennington. op.cit. 116
16   W. S. Perry. The American Episcopal Church. (Boston 1885) Vol. I 3

V ARCHITECTS AND PLANNERS

1   E. W. Thomson. Life of Thomas Bray. (London 1954) gives an interesting account of Bray's ministry in America and subsequently
2   H. P. Thompson. Into All Lands (London 1951) 23
3   Dictionary of America. Biography Vol. V 290
4   H. P. Thompson. op.cit. 26
5   S.P.G. MSS A I 9
6   S.P.G. MSS A I 56
7   S.P.G. MSS A I 183

8   S.P.G. MSS A I 183
9   Keith's Journal. (London 1706) 82-8
10   E. L. Pennington. Apostle of New Jersey 72
       G. M. Hills. History of the Church in Burlington, New Jersey.
       (Trenton N. J. 1885) 27-2

VI SPREADING THE WORD

1   C. F. Pascoe. op.cit. 849-85
2   C. F. Pascoe. op.cit. Cap XII
3   J. K. Nelson. op.cit. page 94 cites a number of instances of anti-Scottish
       prejudice
4   A. P. Middleton. (Ea) Tercentenary Essays Commemorating Maryland
       1692-1792
       (Virginia Beach1992) 6
5   S.P.G. MSS A ii 23
6   E. L. Pennington. The Episcopal Church in Florida. Historical Magazine
       PECUSA
       (Vol. VII 1938) 7
7   G. W. Lamb. Clergymen Licensed to the American Colonies 1745-81
       (Historical Magazine) Vol. VIII 1944 128
8   E. L. Pennington. op.cit. 5
9   E. L. Pennington. op.cit.
10   J. W. Lydekker. The Faithful Mohawks (Cambridge 1938)
11   S.P.G. MSS A ii 122
12   C. F. Pascoe. op.cit. Vol. I 6
13   S.P.G. MSS B ii 363
14   O. Anderson. 400 Years. (Cincinnati 1997) 2
15   Dictionary of American Biography. Vol vi 1

GENERAL NOTES ON CHAPTERS VII, VIII AND IX

Statistical information and brief biographical details of all clergy sent out by the Society for the Propagation of the Gospel can be found in Two Hundred Years of the SPG by C F Pascoe vol ii The Missionary Roll pp 849 ff.

A more comprehensive list (again with some biographical details) can be compiled from four articles appearing in the Historical Magazine of the Protestant Episcopal Church. These are as follows.

i   List of Clergymen Receiving a Bounty for Overseas Service 1680–1688
       Nelson W. Rightmyer, June 1948
ii   List of over 200 Clergymen Licensed by the Bishop of London

for Overseas Service 1696–1710 and 1715–1716
John Clement. December 1947
iii Anglican Clergymen Licensed to the American Colonies 1710–1744
with Biographical Studies
John Clement. September1948
iv List of Clergymen Licensed by the Bishop of London to the American
Colonies 1745–1781
George W. Lamb. June 1944

VII THE SOUTHERN COLONIES

1 Virginia
A Blessed Company.
Parishes, Parsons and Parishioners in Virginia 1690–1776
John K. Nelson. London 2002
Early Days of the Diocese of Virginia
G MacLaran Brydon. Richmond VA 1935
Colonial Churches in the Original Colony of Virginia
W. M. Clark. Editor. Richmond VA 1908
The Diary of Robert Rose – A View of Virginia by a Scottish Colonial
Parson
Ralph E. Fall. Verona VA 1977
Scotus Americanus
W. R. Brock. Edinburgh 1982
(has notes relating to the Rose, Scott and Lang families)

2 Maryland, Delaware and Virginia
Biographical Notes. The Colonial Clergy of Maryland, Delaware and
Georgia
Frederick L. Weis. Lancaster. Mass 1950
The First Parishes of the Province of Maryland
Perry G. Skirven. Baltimore, Maryland 1994
Tercentenary Essays – Anglican Maryland 1692–1792
A. P. Middleton. Virginia Beach 1992
The Character of the Anglican Clergy of Colonial Maryland
Nelson W. Rightmyer. Historical Magazine. June 1950

3 Wesley and Whitefield
Life of the Revd. Charles Wesley. Vols i and ii
J. Whitehead. London 1843

VIII THE MIDDLE COLONIES

1   New York
     Life and Letters of Charles Inglis
     J. W. Lydekker. London 1936
     The Beginnings of the Church in the Province of New York
     E. Clowes Chorley. Historical Magazine 1944

2   New Jersey
     Apostle of New Jersey. John Talbot 1643–1727
     Edgar L. Pennington. Philadelphia 1938
     The Anglican Church in New Jersey
     N. R. Burr. Philadelphia 1954
     History of the Colonial Church
     J. S. M Anderson. London 1876

3   Delaware
     Biographical Notes. The Colonial Clergy of Delaware
     Frederick Weis. Lancaster Mass 1951

IX NEW ENGLAND

1   New England
     New England Clergy in the American Revolution
     C. Mampoteng. Historical Magazine December 1940
     A History of the American Episcopal Church pp 107 ff
     W. W. Manross. New York 1959
     Into All Lands pp 84 ff
     H. P. Thompson. London 1951
     The Reverend Roger Price (1696–1762) Commissary to New England
     1730–1748
     Mary P. Salsman. Historical Magazine September 1945

X ESTABLISHMENT AND THE STRUGGLE FOR THE EPISCOPATE

1   W. R. W. Stephens. Life and Letters of Walter Farquhar Hook.
     (London 1880) vol. I 76
2   H. R. Trevor-Roper. Archbishop Laud. (London 1940) 258
3   F. L. Cross. (Ed) Oxford Dictionary of the Christian Church 176
4   J. R. H. Moorman. History of the Church of England. (London 1954) 250
5   G. R. Cragg. Puritanism in the Period of the Great Persecution.
     (Cambridge 957) 1 ff

6   J. Bramhall. Works. (Oxford 1851) vol. iii 518
7   R. Foskett. Some Scottish Links with the American Episcopal Church.
         (Edinburgh 1962) 11
8   S. P. G. Mss AI 125
9   E. L. Pennington. Apostle of New Jersey 38 –
10   Lambeth Mss 711 Folio 118
11   S. P. G. Mss A viii 181-182
12   S. P. G. Mss A xii 177
13   C. F. Pascoe. op.cit. 746
14   ibid - 747
15   H. G. G. Herklots. Frontiers of the Christian Church. 56 –
16   S. P. G. Mss B ii 57
17   S. Wilberforce. op.cit. 163
18   S. P. G. Anniversary Sermon. London 1771 17 –

XI SOME CONSEQUENCES OF NO BISHOP

1   E. L. Pennington. op.cit. 74 ff
2   J. Whitehead. Life of The Revd. Charles Wesley. (London 1893) vol. ii
         419
3   W. J. Seabury. Memoir of Bishop Seabury. (New York 1908) 376
4   S. Wilberforce. op.cit. 180
5   E. E. Beardsley. Life and Correspondence of Bishop Seabury. (Boston
         1882) 189
6   W. A. Spooner. Bishop Butler (London 1901) 30
7   C. F. Pascoe. op.cit. vol. I 62
8   H. G. Herklots. op.cit. 86
9   W. J. Seabury. op.cit. 116 – 117
10   B. L. Manning. The Protestant Dissenting Deputies. (Cambridge 1952)
         417
11   T. B. Chandler. Life of Samuel Johnson DD. (London 1854) 410
12   C. F. Pascoe. op.cit. vol. ii 848

XII INDEPENDENCE AND ITS CONSEQUENCES

1   J. McVicker. The Early Life and Professional Years of Bishop Hobart
         (Oxford 1838) 215
2   S. Wilberforce. op.cit. 181
3   H. G. Herklots. op.cit. 92
4   E. E. Beardsley. op.cit. 114
5   R. D. Middleton. Dr. Routh 59

6   W. White. The Case of the Episcopal Church in the United States
        Considered
        (Published anonymously) (Philadelphia 1782) 32
7   E. E. Beardsley. op.cit. 87
8   ibid 48
9   B. E. Steiner. Samuel Seabury (Ohio 1971) 193
10   W. J. Seabury. op.cit. 211
11   B. E. Steiner. op.cit. 199- 20
12   Scottish Guardian. 25 April 1874 232
13   W. J. Seabury. op.cit. 229
14   S. Wilberforce. op.cit. 206
15   Seabury Centenary. Connecticut Papers 1874. 51

XIII CONSECRATION OF SAMUEL SEABURY

1   Ms Register of the College of Bishops 1784
2   John Skinner. The Nature and Extent of the Apostolical Commission
        (Aberdeen 1785)
3   M. Lochhead. Episcopal Scotland in the 19th Century. (London 1966) 54
4   Scottish Guardian. 25 April 1884
5   Ms Register of the College of Bishops 1784
6   Scottish Guardian 25 April 1884
7   B. E. Steiner. op.cit. 220
8   Ms Register of the College of Bishops 1785

XIV SEABURY AND AFTER

1   Dictionary of American Biography
2   24 Geo iii cap 35
3   24 Geo iii cap 85
4   Ms Lambeth Palace Chapel Register of Consecrations 1787
5   B. E. Steiner. op.cit 280 – 28
6   W. J. Seabury. op.cit. 250
7   B. E. Steiner. op.cit. 309 – 311
8   E. E. Beardsley. op.cit. 423
9   W. J. Seabury. op.cit. 251
10   H. G. Herklots. op.cit. 101 Ibid 112 3 Victoria c 33
11   J. D. Mowat. Bishop A. P. Forbes (Edinburgh 1925) 21
12   M. Russell. History of the Protestant Episcopal Church in The United
        States of America.
        (London 1844) 284 15 ibid 268 16 F. L. Hawk. Memorials (Maryland 1839) 210

Edward Luscombe was Bishop of Brechin in the Scottish Episcopal Church for fifteen years and Primus from 1985 to 1990. He is an Honorary Canon of Trinity Cathedral Iowa, and was made an Honorary Research Fellow of the University of Dundee in 1993.